CHILDREN'S
WORLD
ATLAS

igloo

Published in 2009
by Igloo Books Ltd
Cottage Farm
Sywell
NN6 0BJ
www.igloo-books.com

10 9 8 7 6 5 4 3 2 1

ISBN: 978 1 84817 648 5

Project Managed by HL Studios, Long Hanborough, Oxon

Printed and manufactured in China

CHILDREN'S
WORLD
ATLAS

EXPLORE EVERY CORNER OF OUR PLANET!

Contents

Europe

The Americas

Africa

Asia

Australia-Oceania

The Poles

How to get the best out

The world map is shaded purple to show where the country is located.

This atlas covers both whole continents as well as individual countries. The six main continents of the world are – North America, South America, Europe, Asia, Africa and Australasia-Oceania.

Use the country pages to learn about the geography and people of different places. Every country is famous for something – check out the Fascinating Facts panels – covering everything from the world's heaviest ever pear to the longest snake!

Data Bank

See at a glance the longest river, the highest mountain, how many people there are and how wealthy the country is.

Flip from page to page to compare how these facts change from place to place and continent to continent.

Australia

While a large proportion of inland Australia is desert, 40% of Australia enjoys a tropical climate and snow falls in the Australian Alps at the south end of the Great Dividing Range, or Eastern Highlands. This is Australia's most substantial range of mountains, which stretches from the north-eastern Queensland into the central plain in western Victoria.

DATA BANK

Longest river
Murray 1,566 miles (2,520 km)

Highest mountain
Mount Kosciuszko 7,313 ft (2,229 m)

Coastline
16,007 miles (25,760 km)

Climate
Very dry in centre, mild in south and east, tropical in north.

Largest city and population
Sydney 4,000,000

Annual income
US $31,900 or £18,000 approx. per person

The Alice Springs School of the Air provides an educational service for children living in settlements covering over 386,000 sq miles (1 million sq km) of central Australia. These children live in an isolated environment, and their school classes were conducted via shortwave radio until very recently. Today most schools use wireless internet links to receive their lessons.

116

Finally, look at the splendid photographs which show just what a wonderful world it is in which we live. From deserts to rainforest, ice caps to tropical beaches, our natural world is truly breathtaking. Humans, too, have built magnificent structures, from ancient monuments such as The Great Wall of China and the Pyramids of Egypt, to the Space Shuttle and the skyscrapers of Hong Kong.

# of this atlas

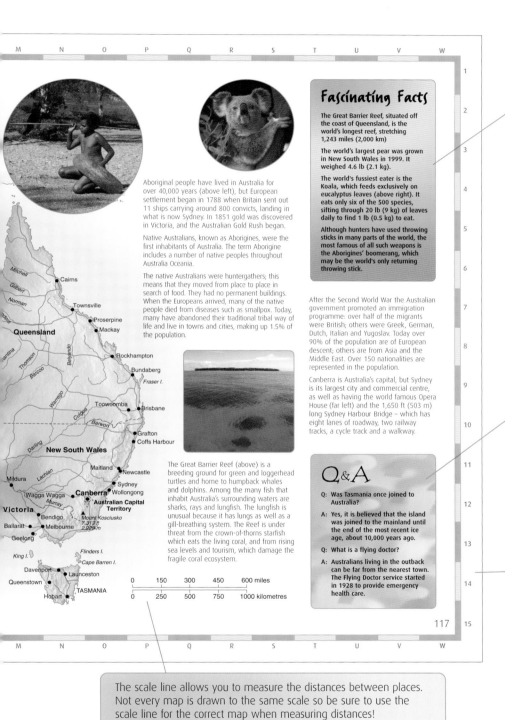

Aboriginal people have lived in Australia for over 40,000 years (above left), but European settlement began in 1788 when Britain sent out 11 ships carrying around 800 convicts, landing in what is now Sydney. In 1851 gold was discovered in Victoria, and the Australian Gold Rush began.

Native Australians, known as Aborigines, were the first inhabitants of Australia. The term Aborigine includes a number of native peoples throughout Australia Oceania.

The native Australians were huntergathers; this means that they moved from place to place in search of food. They had no permanent buildings. When the Europeans arrived, many of the native people died from diseases such as smallpox. Today, many have abandoned their traditional tribal way of life and live in towns and cities, making up 1.5% of the population.

The Great Barrier Reef (above) is a breeding ground for green and loggerhead turtles and home to humpback whales and dolphins. Among the many fish that inhabit Australia's surrounding waters are sharks, rays and lungfish. The lungfish is unusual because it has lungs as well as a gill-breathing system. The Reef is under threat from the crown-of-thorns starfish which eats the living coral, and from rising sea levels and tourism, which damage the fragile coral ecosystem.

After the Second World War the Australian government promoted an immigration programme: over half of the migrants were British; others were Greek, German, Dutch, Italian and Yugoslav. Today over 90% of the population are of European descent; others are from Asia and the Middle East. Over 150 nationalities are represented in the population.

Canberra is Australia's capital, but Sydney is its largest city and commercial centre, as well as having the world famous Opera House (far left) and the 1,650 ft (503 m) long Sydney Harbour Bridge – which has eight lanes of roadway, two railway tracks, a cycle track and a walkway.

Fascinating Facts

The Great Barrier Reef, situated off the coast of Queensland, is the world's longest reef, stretching 1,243 miles (2,000 km)

The world's largest pear was grown in New South Wales in 1999. It weighed 4.6 lb (2.1 kg).

The world's fussiest eater is the Koala, which feeds exclusively on eucalyptus leaves (above right). It eats only six of the 500 species, sifting through 20 lb (9 kg) of leaves daily to find 1 lb (0.5 kg) to eat.

Although hunters have used throwing sticks in many parts of the world, the most famous of all such weapons is the Aborigines' boomerang, which may be the world's only returning throwing stick.

Q&A

Q: Was Tasmania once joined to Australia?

A: Yes, it is believed that the island was joined to the mainland until the end of the most recent ice age, about 10,000 years ago.

Q: What is a flying doctor?

A: Australians living in the outback can be far from the nearest town. The Flying Doctor service started in 1928 to provide emergency health care.

0 150 300 450 600 miles
0 250 500 750 1000 kilometres

117

Fascinating Facts

Fascinating facts boxes contain information that might be: surprising; unbelievable; charming; delightful; intriguing. The information should make you want to know more about the fact. For instance how many times does the Nullarbor train stop on its 297 mile (478 km) journey across the Nullabor plain?

Q & A

The Questions and Answers boxes contain some quite simple questions – you might know the answer before you read it! That partly depends where you live. If you live in Australia you might know the answer to Australian questions, but you may not if you live in Canada or Scotland. But you'll perhaps know the answers to the Scottish or Canadian questions. Some of the questions are more difficult, and you may not even know the answers if they're about your own country.

Using Grid References

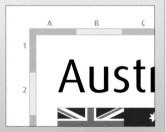

You can use the letters and numbers around the map to locate places listed in the index. For example, Canberra, the capital of Australia, has a reference of 117 O12. This means page 117, column O, Row 12.

The scale line allows you to measure the distances between places. Not every map is drawn to the same scale so be sure to use the scale line for the correct map when measuring distances!

0 150 300 450 600 miles
0 250 500 750 1000 kilometres

Earth and Sun
The seasons

Unless you live on the equator, summer days
have more daylight than winter days. Summer
is warmer than winter. You know this is true,
but do you know why?

The equator

Imagine the Earth is a ball, or a globe. The area at the very top is
the North Pole, and the area at the bottom is the South Pole. The
equator is a line that goes horizontally around the Earth, halfway
between the North Pole and the South Pole. You can see this line
on the globes in the diagram. We use this line as a measuring tool.

The two poles are the coldest places on the Earth, and the
equator is the hottest place.

The hemispheres

There are two hemispheres – they are the Northern Hemisphere
and the Southern Hemisphere. Everywhere north of the equator
is in the Northern Hemisphere and everywhere south of the
equator is in the Southern Hemisphere.

We often speak about he Northern and Southern hemispheres,
but there are Eastern and Western Hemispheres too. That is why
we talk about the East and the West when we're discussing the
various parts of the world.

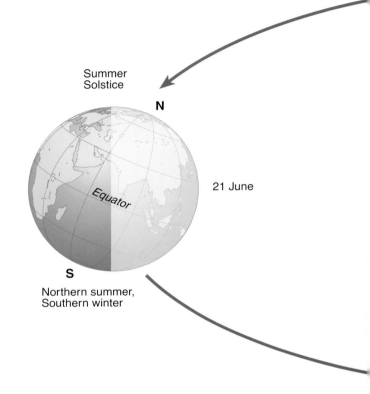

Sp
eq

Summer
Solstice

N

21 June

Equator

S

Northern summer,
Southern winter

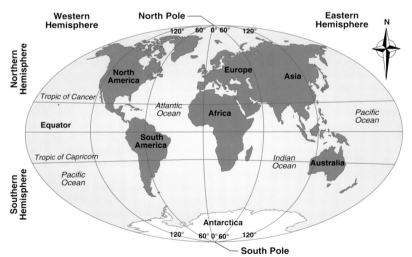

The earth tilts. From April to September
the Northern Hemisphere is tilted towards
the sun and receives more sunlight than
the Southern Hemisphere. This is the
northern summer and the southern
winter. In the Arctic Circle the sun does
not set, and the North Pole has six
months of uninterrupted daylight. From
October to March the Southern
Hemisphere is tilted towards the sun and
receives more sunlight than the Northern
Hemisphere. This is the southern summer
and the northern winter. In the Antarctic
Circle the sun does not set, and the South
Pole has six months of uninterrupted
daylight. The North Pole is now in
darkness for six months.

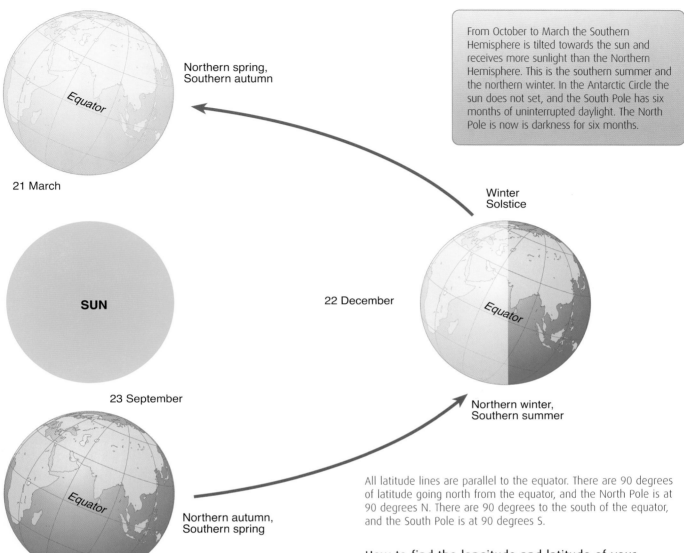

Northern spring,
Southern autumn

Equator

21 March

From October to March the Southern
Hemisphere is tilted towards the sun and
receives more sunlight than the Northern
Hemisphere. This is the southern summer and
the northern winter. In the Antarctic Circle the
sun does not set, and the South Pole has six
months of uninterrupted daylight. The North
Pole is now is darkness for six months.

Winter
Solstice

SUN

22 December

Equator

23 September

Northern winter,
Southern summer

Northern autumn,
Southern spring

Equator

All latitude lines are parallel to the equator. There are 90 degrees
of latitude going north from the equator, and the North Pole is at
90 degrees N. There are 90 degrees to the south of the equator,
and the South Pole is at 90 degrees S.

How to find the longitude and latitude of your own town

Any place in the world can be described with just two numbers, its
latitude and longitude. Each degree of latitude or longitude is further
sub-divided into 60 minutes. One minute of latitude is one nautical
mile, or 1,852 metres. One minute of latitude can be further divided
into 60 seconds. These numbers are used by aircraft, ships, and
anyone with a GPS (global positioning system) device.

So how does it work?

Look up your town on a map that has the latitude and longitude
lines marked. Mark the point where your town is and see where
this fits with the lines going vertically – up and down (longitude)
and the lines going horizontally – across (latitude). Where the
lines meet is the latitude and longitude of your home town.

Example: The Taj Mahal, India: Latitude: 27° 10' 25.09" N and
Longitude: 78° 2' 32.9" E. We have to say either N or S for North
and South because, for instance, the equator is 0°. There can
then be a 40° line north or south. Similarly we include E and W
for the longitude positions.

Longitude

Longitude lines run vertically around the globe and they all go
through both poles. The longitude line with the value of 0 runs
through Greenwich in England. It is called the Prime Meridian, and
it does the same job as the equator. Longitude lines show the
distance between the Prime Meridian and any point east or west
of it. There are 180 degrees of longitude to the east of the Prime
Meridian, and 180 degrees of longitude to the west of it.

Once you have all these lines of measurement, you can find any
place marked on a map!

Latitude

The line that we call the equator is a latitude line, and it has a
value of 0 degrees. This means it is the starting point for
measuring latitude. Latitude lines show the distance between the
equator and anywhere north or south of it.

The Earth in space

Uranus is very cold, as it is 20 times further from the heat of the Sun than the Earth.

Mercury is the closest planet to the Sun and is the fastest-moving planet. Temperatures on Mercury range between 750°F –274°F (400°C and –170°C).

Mars also has an atmosphere and has, in the past, had water, leading to theories that there might be life on Mars. Space probes have tested the surface and found no trace of life.

Saturn is famous for its rings, which are 167,000 miles (270,000 km) across but only 660 ft (200m) thick. The rings are made of chunks of ice varying from snowball to iceberg size.

Earth looks blue and white from space due to the oceans and clouds which cover its surface. It consists of a solid crust above a molten layer, at the centre of which is a solid iron core. Earth is surrounded by a layer of gases which form an atmosphere, and 71% of its surface is covered with liquid water – a property unique to the Solar System and which has enabled life to develop. The earth is 94.5 million miles (152 million km) from the sun.

Jupiter is the largest planet. It consists of hydrogen and helium and is covered by clouds.

Venus is a similar size to the Earth; it is the brightest and, at 475°C, the hottest of the planets, due to its atmosphere of carbon dioxide gas which traps the Sun's energy. Scientists have tried to send probes onto this scorching planet, but the atmosphere has proved too hot.

ne was little-known until the er 2 spacecraft showed es of its blue-green clouds.

Pluto is the smallest, coldest and most distant planet in the Solar System and was only discovered in 1930. Surface temperatures are −387.5°F (−233°C).

World
Political

The division of the world into countries is constantly developing and the world map is always changing. In recent times Eastern Europe has seen the rise of a number of small nations following the break-up of the old Soviet Union. Parts of Africa and Asia have also become independent countries.

The ten largest countries in the world by area are:

1. Russia 6,592,771 sq miles (17,075,200 sq km)
2. Canada 3,851,809 sq miles (9,976,140 sq km)
3. U.S.A. 3,717,812 sq miles (9,629,091 sq km)
4. China 3,705,406 sq miles (9,596,960 sq km)
5. Brazil 3,286,488 sq miles (8,511,965 sq km)
6. Australia 2,967,909 sq miles (7,686,850 sq km)
7. India 1,269,345 sq miles (3,287,590 sq km)
8. Argentina 1,068,302 sq miles (2,766,890 sq km)
9. Kazakhstan 1,049,155 sq miles (2,717,300 sq km)
10. Sudan 967,498 sq miles (2,505,810 sq km)

Although Russia is the largest country in the world by area, it isn't the most highly populated. It is eighth on the list of most highly populated countries. China and India head the list for the highest population, followed by the United States.

The ten smallest countries in the world by area are:

1. Holy See (Vatican City) 0.17 sq miles (0.44 sq km)
2. Monaco 0.75 sq miles (1.95 sq km)
3. Nauru 8 sq miles (21 sq km)
4. Tuvalu 10 sq miles (26 sq km)
5. San Marino 24 sq miles (61 sq km)
6. Liechtenstein 62 sq miles (160 sq km)
7. Marshall Islands 70 sq miles (181 sq km)
8. Seychelles 104 sq miles (270 sq km)
9. Maldives 116 sq miles (300 sq km)
10. St. Kitts and Nevis 139 sq miles (360 sq km)

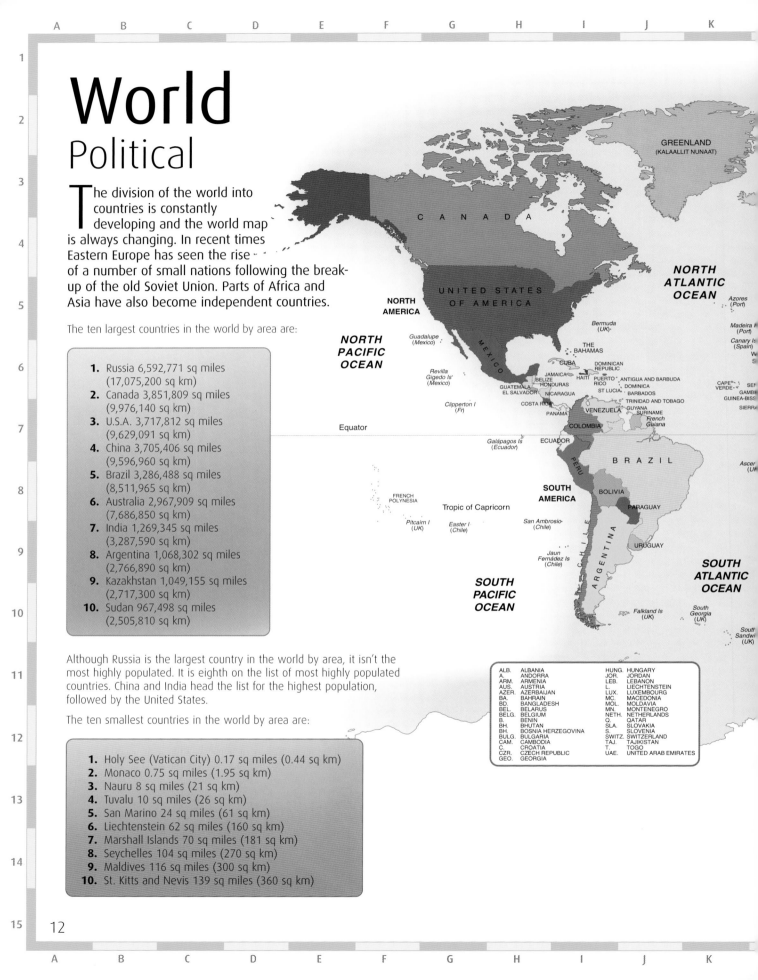

NORTH AMERICA

NORTH PACIFIC OCEAN

CANADA

UNITED STATES OF AMERICA

MEXICO

GREENLAND (KALAALLIT NUNAAT)

NORTH ATLANTIC OCEAN

Azores (Port)

Madeira (Port)

Canary Is (Spain)

Bermuda (UK)

Guadalupe (Mexico)

THE BAHAMAS

CUBA

DOMINICAN REPUBLIC

Revilla Gigedo Is (Mexico)

JAMAICA   HAITI   PUERTO   ANTIGUA AND BARBUDA
BELIZE   RICO
GUATEMALA HONDURAS   ST LUCIA   DOMINICA
EL SALVADOR NICARAGUA   BARBADOS

CAPE VERDE

SEN
GAMBI
GUINEA-BISS

SIERRA

Clipperton I (Fr)

COSTA RICA   TRINIDAD AND TOBAGO

PANAMA   VENEZUELA   GUYANA   SURINAME
                              French
COLOMBIA   Guiana

Equator

Galápagos Is (Ecuador)   ECUADOR

PERU

BRAZIL

Ascer (UK

FRENCH POLYNESIA

SOUTH AMERICA

Tropic of Capricorn

BOLIVIA

PARAGUAY

Pitcairn I (UK)

Easter I (Chile)

San Ambrosio (Chile)

Jaun Fernádez Is (Chile)

CHILE   ARGENTINA   URUGUAY

SOUTH ATLANTIC OCEAN

SOUTH PACIFIC OCEAN

Falkland Is (UK)

South Georgia (UK)

South Sandwi (UK)

ALB.	ALBANIA	HUNG.	HUNGARY
A.	ANDORRA	JOR.	JORDAN
ARM.	ARMENIA	LEB.	LEBANON
AUS.	AUSTRIA	L.	LIECHTENSTEIN
AZER.	AZERBAIJAN	LUX.	LUXEMBOURG
BA.	BAHRAIN	MC.	MACEDONIA
BD.	BANGLADESH	MOL.	MOLDAVIA
BEL.	BELARUS	MN.	MONTENEGRO
BELG.	BELGIUM	NETH.	NETHERLANDS
B.	BENIN	Q.	QATAR
BH.	BHUTAN	SLA.	SLOVAKIA
BH.	BOSNIA HERZEGOVINA	S.	SLOVENIA
BULG.	BULGARIA	SWITZ.	SWITZERLAND
CAM.	CAMBODIA	TAJ.	TAJIKISTAN
C.	CROATIA	T.	TOGO
CZR.	CZECH REPUBLIC	UAE.	UNITED ARAB EMIRATES
GEO.	GEORGIA		

ARCTIC OCEAN

CTIC
EAN

Franz Joseph Land

Svalbard
(Nor)

N
O
R
W
A
Y

S
W
E
D
E
N

FINLAND

DENMARK

ESTONIA
LATVIA
LITH.
BELARUS

NETH.
GERMANY
BELG.
POLAND
LUX
CZR.
SLA
FRANCE
SWITZ.
AUS. HUNG.
MOL.
ROMANIA
BH SERBIA
MN.
BULG.
ALB.
GREECE

ITALY

RUSSIA

KAZAKHSTAN

Caspian
Sea

Black Sea

GEO.
ARM. AZER.

LOR MONIA

KYRGYZSTAN

TURKMENISTAN

TAJ.

MONGOLIA

CHINA

NORTH
KOREA
SOUTH
KOREA

JAPAN

NORTH
AMERICA

Aleutian Islands
(USA)

NORTH
PACIFIC
OCEAN

TURKEY

MALTA

CYPRUS
LEB
ISRAEL

SYRIA

IRAQ

IRAN

AFGHANISTAN

PAKISTAN

NEPAL

BH.

BD

MYANMAR
(BURMA)

LAOS

Taiwan

Hong Kong

Marcus
(Japan)

Mariana Is
(USA)

Guam
(USA)

Midway
(USA)

H A W A I I
(USA)

Hawaii

Wake I
(USA)

Johnston Atoll
(USA)

Mediterranean Sea

ERIA

LIBYA

EGYPT

SAUDI
ARABIA

KUWAIT

JOR.

SA
UAE

OMAN

INDIA

SRI
LANKA

THAILAND

CAM

VIETNAM

ASIA

PHILIPPINES

MARSHALL IS

FEDERATED STATES OF
MICRONESIA

Gilbert
Islands

Line Is

LI
NIGER
CHAD
SUDAN

YEMEN

ERITREA
DJIBOUTI

Socotra
(Yemen)

Laccadive Is
(India)

MALDIVES

BRUNEI

SINGAPORE

MALAYSIA

PALAU

NGERIA

CAMEROON

CENTRAL AFRICAN
REPUBLIC

ETHIOPIA

SOMALIA

KENYA

INDONESIA

PAPUA NEW
GUINEA

NAURU

KIRIBATI

Phoenix
Islands

Marquesas
Tuamotu
Archipelago

EQUATORIAL
GUINEA
SAO TOME &
PRINCIPE

GABON

CONGO

CONGO
(DEMOCRATIC
REPUBLIC)

RWANDA
BURUNDI

UGANDA

TANZANIA

SEYCHELLES

SOLOMON
ISLANDS

TOKELAU Is
(NZ)

ANGOLA

ZAMBIA

MALAWI

COMOROS

INDIAN
OCEAN

Christmas I
(Aust)

Keeling I
(Aust)

TUVALU

WESTERN
SAMOA

AMERICAN
SAMOA

NAMIBIA

ZIMBABWE

BOTSWANA

MOZAMBIQUE

MAURITIUS

Réunion
(Fr)

VANUATU

New
Caledonia
(Fr)

FIJI

TONGA

Niue
(NZ)

Cook Is
(NZ)

FRENCH
POLYNESIA

SWAZILAND

SOUTH
AFRICA

LESOTHO

MADAGASCAR

AUSTRALIA

AUSTRALASIA

Kermadec Is
(NZ)

unha

St Paul I
(Fr.)

NEW
ZEALAND

Crozet Is
(Fr.)

Prince Edward Is
(S. Af.)

Kerguelen I
(Fr.)

Chatham Is
(NZ)

vet I
way)

Heard I
(Aust.)

0	600	1200	1800	2400 miles
0	1000	2000	3000	4000 kilometres

Drawing the world on a flat map
distorts distances. The scale line is
only accurate at the Equator

Macquarie
(Aust)

ANTARCTICA

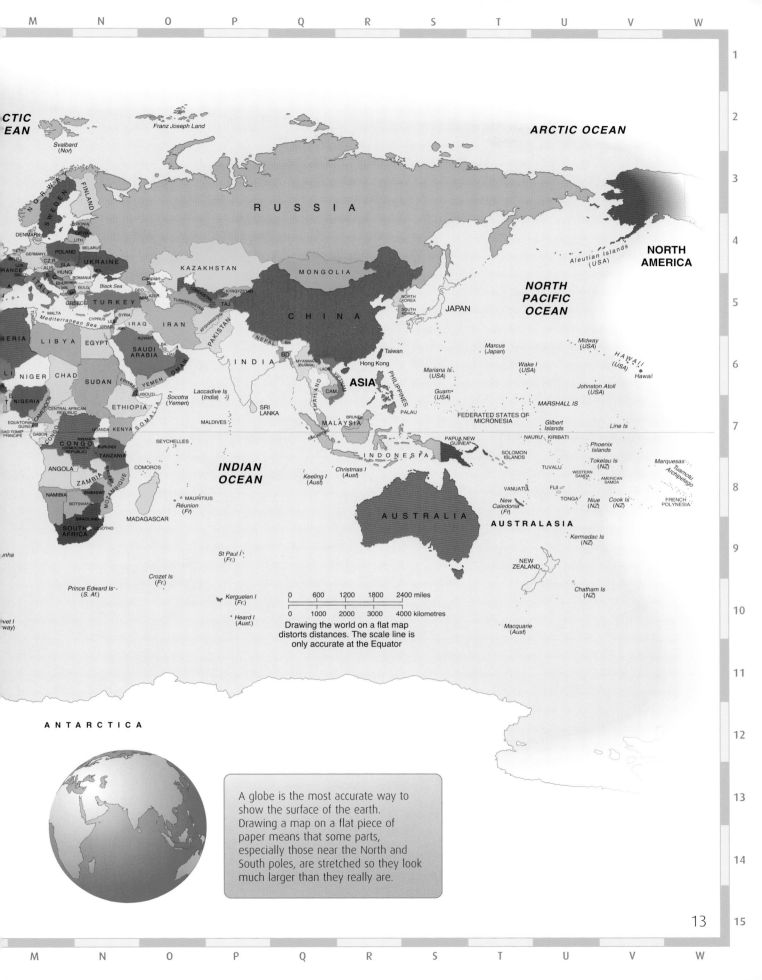

A globe is the most accurate way to
show the surface of the earth.
Drawing a map on a flat piece of
paper means that some parts,
especially those near the North and
South poles, are stretched so they look
much larger than they really are.

World
Landscape

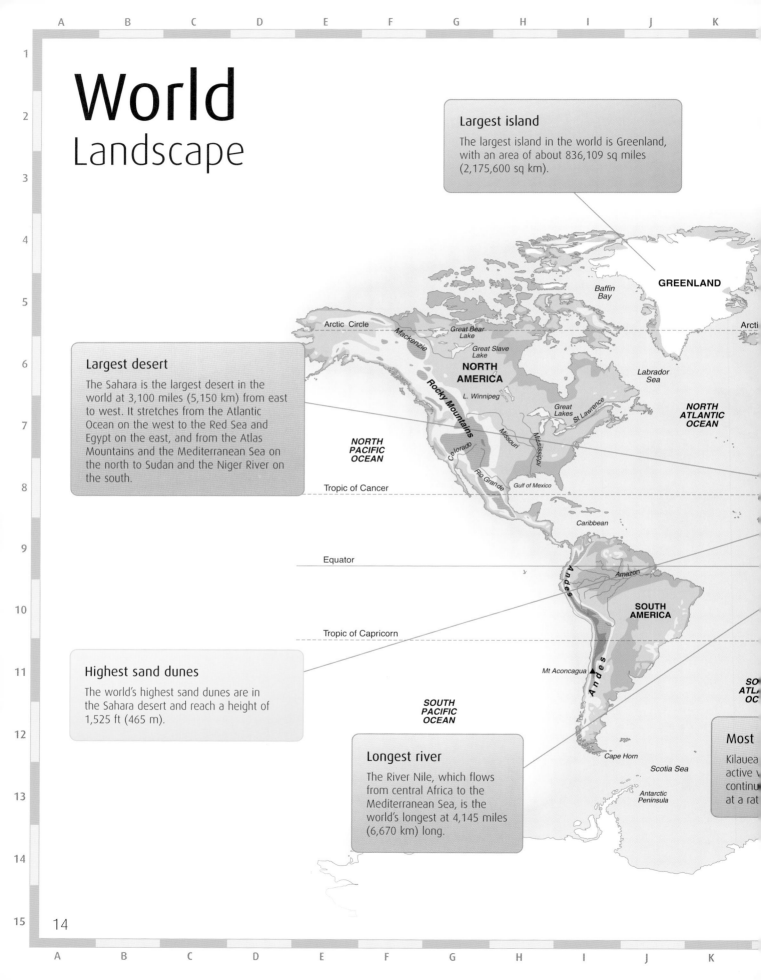

Largest island

The largest island in the world is Greenland, with an area of about 836,109 sq miles (2,175,600 sq km).

GREENLAND

Baffin
Bay

Arctic Circle

Arcti

Great Bear
Lake

Mackenzie

Great Slave
Lake

**NORTH
AMERICA**

Labrador
Sea

**NORTH
ATLANTIC
OCEAN**

L. Winnipeg

Rocky Mountains

Missouri

St Lawrence

Great
Lakes

Mississippi

**NORTH
PACIFIC
OCEAN**

Colorado

Rio Grande

Gulf of Mexico

Tropic of Cancer

Caribbean

Equator

Andes

Amazon

**SOUTH
AMERICA**

Tropic of Capricorn

Mt Aconcagua ▲

Andes

SO
ATL
OC

Largest desert

The Sahara is the largest desert in the world at 3,100 miles (5,150 km) from east to west. It stretches from the Atlantic Ocean on the west to the Red Sea and Egypt on the east, and from the Atlas Mountains and the Mediterranean Sea on the north to Sudan and the Niger River on the south.

Highest sand dunes

The world's highest sand dunes are in the Sahara desert and reach a height of 1,525 ft (465 m).

**SOUTH
PACIFIC
OCEAN**

Cape Horn

Scotia Sea

Antarctic
Peninsula

Longest river

The River Nile, which flows from central Africa to the Mediterranean Sea, is the world's longest at 4,145 miles (6,670 km) long.

Most

Kilauea
active
continu
at a rat

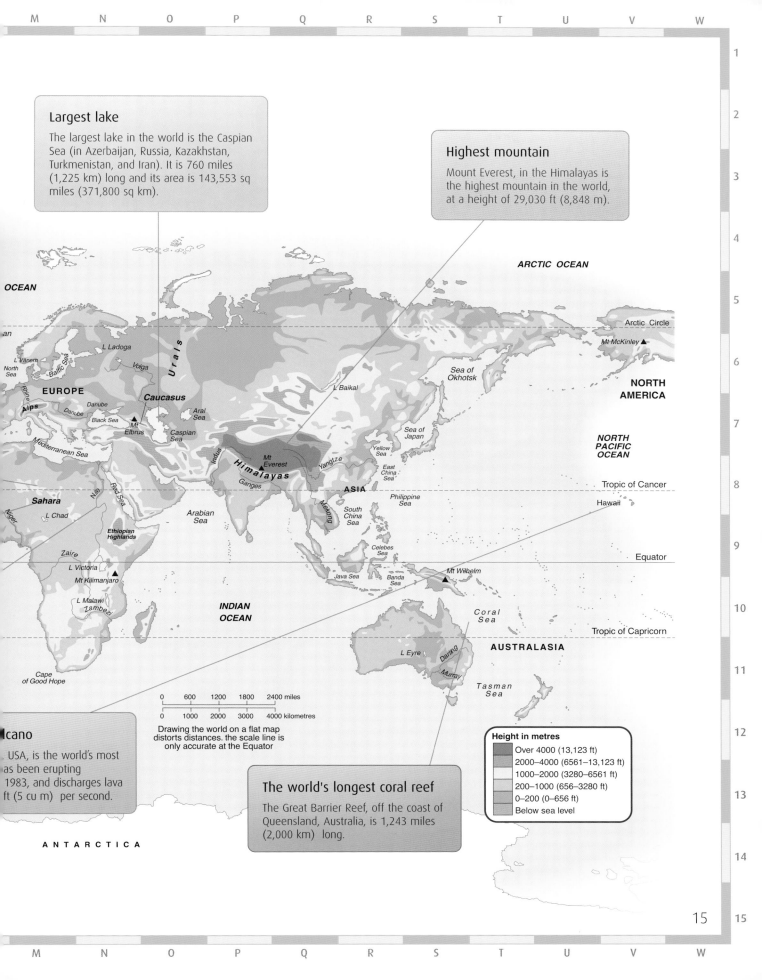

Largest lake

The largest lake in the world is the Caspian Sea (in Azerbaijan, Russia, Kazakhstan, Turkmenistan, and Iran). It is 760 miles (1,225 km) long and its area is 143,553 sq miles (371,800 sq km).

Highest mountain

Mount Everest, in the Himalayas is the highest mountain in the world, at a height of 29,030 ft (8,848 m).

lcano

. USA, is the world's most
as been erupting
1983, and discharges lava
ft (5 cu m) per second.

The world's longest coral reef

The Great Barrier Reef, off the coast of Queensland, Australia, is 1,243 miles (2,000 km) long.

0 600 1200 1800 2400 miles	
0 1000 2000 3000 4000 kilometres	

Drawing the world on a flat map distorts distances. the scale line is only accurate at the Equator

Height in metres

- Over 4000 (13,123 ft)
- 2000–4000 (6561–13,123 ft)
- 1000–2000 (3280–6561 ft)
- 200–1000 (656–3280 ft)
- 0–200 (0–656 ft)
- Below sea level

Map labels: OCEAN, ARCTIC OCEAN, Arctic Circle, Mt McKinley, NORTH AMERICA, NORTH PACIFIC OCEAN, Tropic of Cancer, Hawaii, Equator, Tropic of Capricorn, L Ladoga, L Vänern, North Sea, Baltic Sea, Volga, Urals, L Baikal, Sea of Okhotsk, Sea of Japan, EUROPE, Alps, Rhine, Danube, Caucasus, Mt Elbrus, Black Sea, Aral Sea, Caspian Sea, Mediterranean Sea, Yellow Sea, East China Sea, Indus, Himalayas, Mt Everest, Ganges, Yangtze, ASIA, Philippine Sea, Nile, Red Sea, Sahara, L Chad, Niger, Arabian Sea, Mekong, South China Sea, Ethiopian Highlands, Celebes Sea, Zaire, L Victoria, Mt Kilimanjaro, Java Sea, Banda Sea, Mt Wilhelm, INDIAN OCEAN, L Malawi, Zambezi, Coral Sea, L Eyre, Darling, Murray, AUSTRALASIA, Tasman Sea, Cape of Good Hope, ANTARCTICA

World
Climate

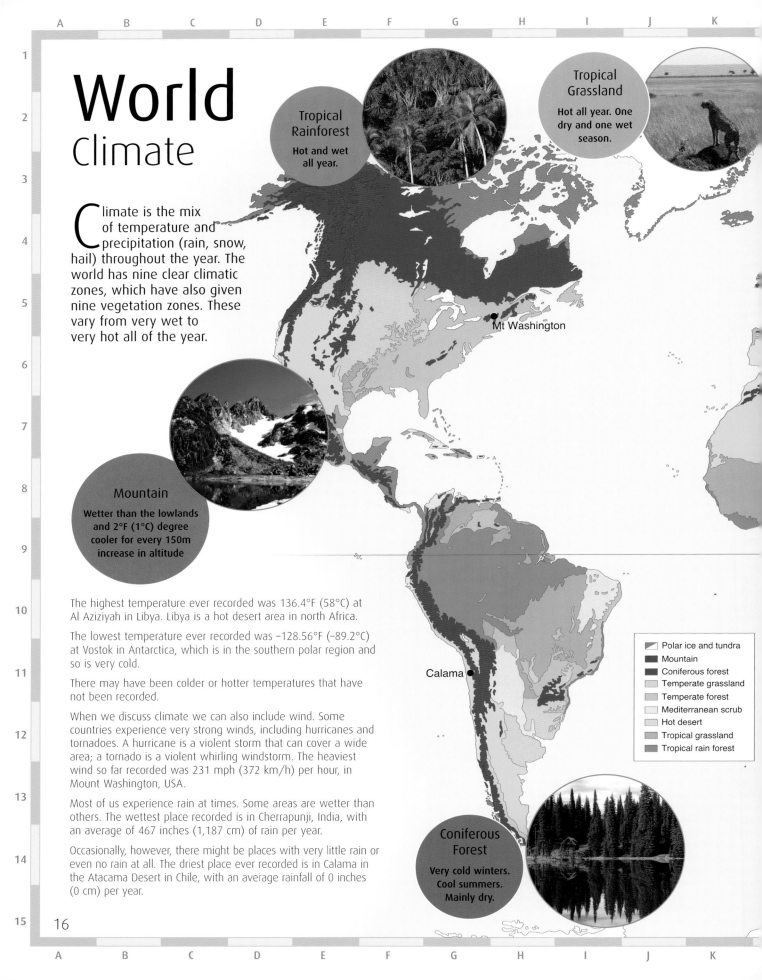

Tropical Rainforest

Hot and wet all year.

Tropical Grassland

Hot all year. One dry and one wet season.

Climate is the mix of temperature and precipitation (rain, snow, hail) throughout the year. The world has nine clear climatic zones, which have also given nine vegetation zones. These vary from very wet to very hot all of the year.

Mt Washington

Mountain

Wetter than the lowlands and 2°F (1°C) degree cooler for every 150m increase in altitude

The highest temperature ever recorded was 136.4°F (58°C) at Al Aziziyah in Libya. Libya is a hot desert area in north Africa.

The lowest temperature ever recorded was −128.56°F (−89.2°C) at Vostok in Antarctica, which is in the southern polar region and so is very cold.

There may have been colder or hotter temperatures that have not been recorded.

When we discuss climate we can also include wind. Some countries experience very strong winds, including hurricanes and tornadoes. A hurricane is a violent storm that can cover a wide area; a tornado is a violent whirling windstorm. The heaviest wind so far recorded was 231 mph (372 km/h) per hour, in Mount Washington, USA.

Most of us experience rain at times. Some areas are wetter than others. The wettest place recorded is in Cherrapunji, India, with an average of 467 inches (1,187 cm) of rain per year.

Occasionally, however, there might be places with very little rain or even no rain at all. The driest place ever recorded is in Calama in the Atacama Desert in Chile, with an average rainfall of 0 inches (0 cm) per year.

Calama

	Polar ice and tundra
	Mountain
	Coniferous forest
	Temperate grassland
	Temperate forest
	Mediterranean scrub
	Hot desert
	Tropical grassland
	Tropical rain forest

Coniferous Forest

Very cold winters. Cool summers. Mainly dry.

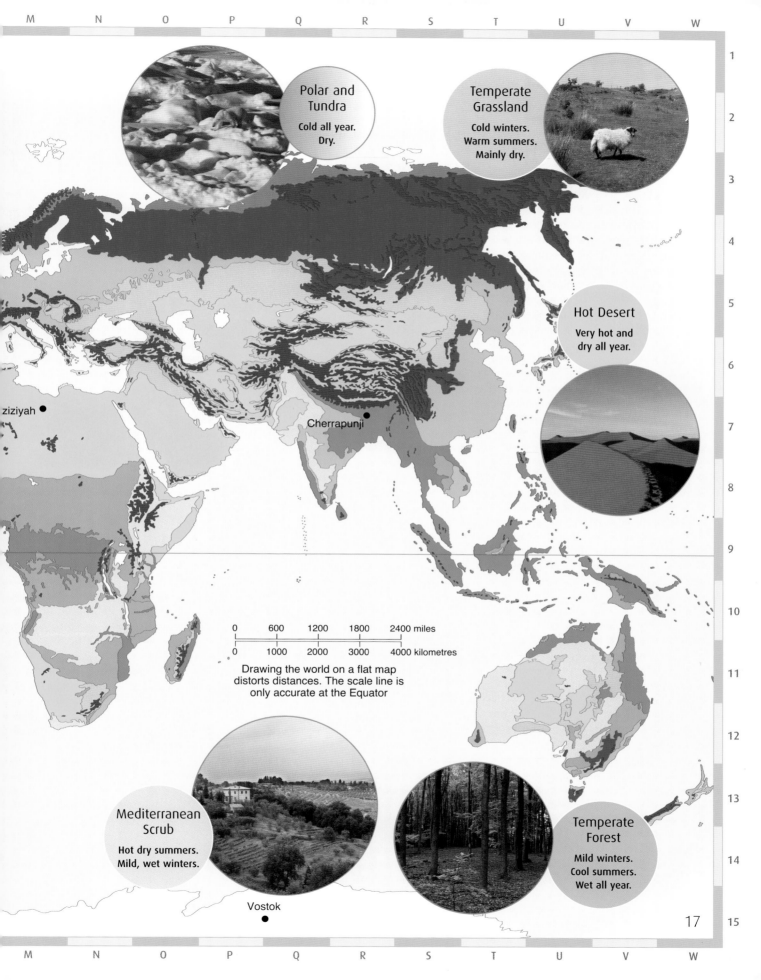

Polar and Tundra

Cold all year.
Dry.

Temperate Grassland

Cold winters.
Warm summers.
Mainly dry.

Hot Desert

Very hot and
dry all year.

ziziyah ●

Cherrapunji ●

0   600   1200   1800   2400 miles

0   1000   2000   3000   4000 kilometres

Drawing the world on a flat map
distorts distances. The scale line is
only accurate at the Equator

**Mediterranean
Scrub**

Hot dry summers.
Mild, wet winters.

**Temperate
Forest**

Mild winters.
Cool summers.
Wet all year.

Vostok
●

17

World Population

People live where conditions favour life. So areas with a climate suited to agriculture will attract people, but at a low density, and areas that have lots of employment, such as cities and industrial regions, have a high population density. Unlike high mountains, deserts, ice caps and very thick forest areas that have very few inhabitants.

However, there are many parts of the world that have a high density of population concentrated in places subject to regular natural disasters, e.g. around flood plains, active volcanos and fault lines where earthquakes are regular. This is because these areas also tend to be very fertile. Bangladesh and Japan are two examples. Bangladesh experiences major flooding almost annually during the monsoon season and Japan has frequent earthquakes, but both are very densely populated. Some countries have a large population but not always a great population density. A look at the population map will show that the densest populations are mostly concentrated in Asia and Europe.

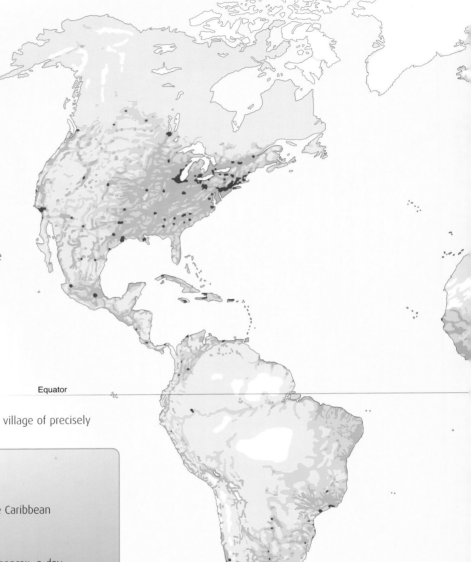

Equator

If we could shrink the world's population to a village of precisely 100 people it would look like this:

- 61 would be Asian
- 13 would be Africans
- 12 would be Europeans
- 9 would be from South America and the Caribbean
- 5 would be from the U.S.A. and Canada
- 75 would be non-white
- 25 would be white
- 48 would live on less than US $2 or £1 approx. a day
- 48 would lack access to basic sanitation
- 47 would live in towns or cities
- 25 would live in sub standard housing or have no home at all
- 17 would be under 18 years old
- 16 would lack access to safe drinking water
- 16 would be unable to read or write
- 14 would suffer from malnutrion
- 8 would have access to the internet from home
- Only 1 would have a college education

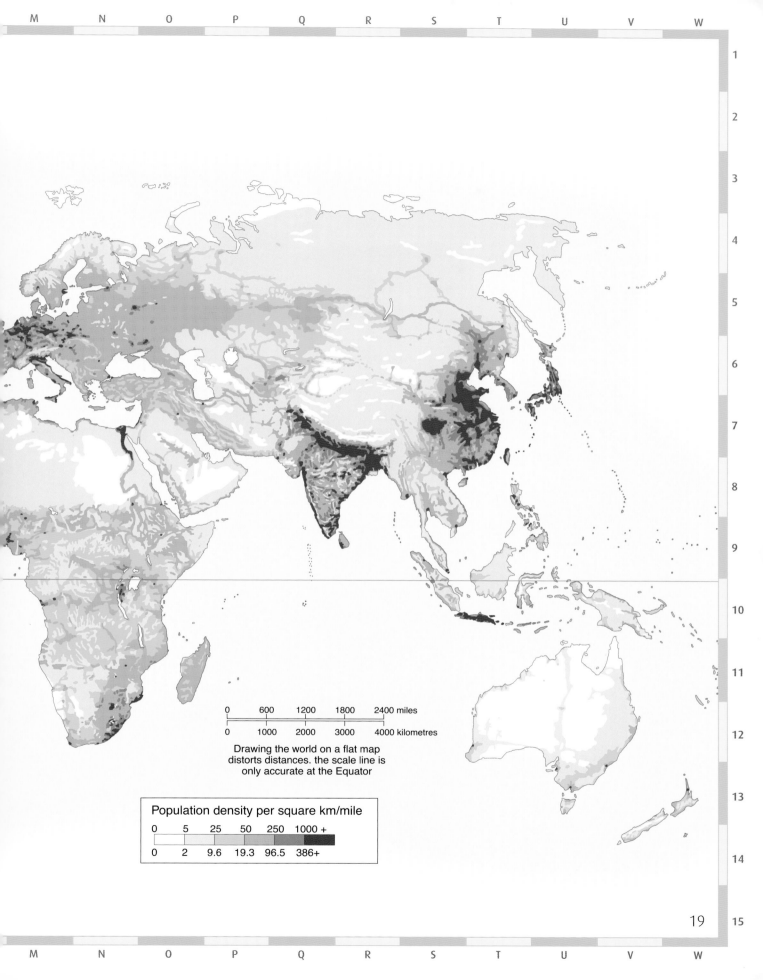

Population density per square km/mile

| 0 | 5 | 25 | 50 | 250 | 1000 + |

| 0 | 2 | 9.6 | 19.3 | 96.5 | 386+ |

0   600   1200   1800   2400 miles

0   1000   2000   3000   4000 kilometres

Drawing the world on a flat map
distorts distances. the scale line is
only accurate at the Equator

World
Rich and Poor

Highest cost of living
Oslo, the capital of Norway, has the highest cost of living in the world.

Lowest cost of living
Tehran, the capital of Iran, has the lowest cost of living in the world.

The world's wealth is very unequally distributed. Millions of people live on less than US $1 (or 60p) per day. Imagine how you would live with so little to provide shelter, food and clothing.

The poorest countries tend to have an unsuitable climate for growing crops or keeping animals, and often have a history of violence and war; many people are not educated.

The wealthiest countries are usually rich in natural rescources, politically stable, and have a climate suited to agriculture and industry, as well as a highly educated population.

So who *really* are the *really* rich and very poor?

Luxemburg is the world's richest nation with over US $56,000 (or £30,000) approx. per person annual income. The richest 20 countries includes 15 European nations, the United States, Canada, Bermuda and Australia.

Eithiopia is the world's poorest nation with under US $100 (or £54) approx. per person annual income. The poorest 20 countries include 17 African nations, and Gaza, Nepal and Tajikstan.

A great many nations are poor because their economies depend upon one cash crop which, if the harvest fails, brings disaster. Then a vicious circle is created which is very difficult to reverse. However the countries that are fortunate enough to have very rich oil and gas reserves have been able to become very wealthy in spite of only having one raw material to trade. This is because the rich countries depend on oil to power their economies. Saudi Arabia is home to 10% of the world's known oil supplies and has prospered in spite of having a harsh climate. Many of the poor countries may have rich mineral wealth, but, because they do not control the mining companies, they are not able to benefit financially from the exploitation of these rescources.

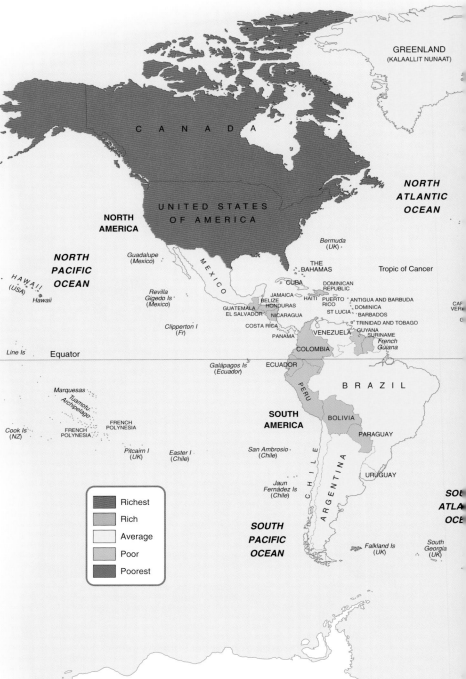

Richest
Rich
Average
Poor
Poorest

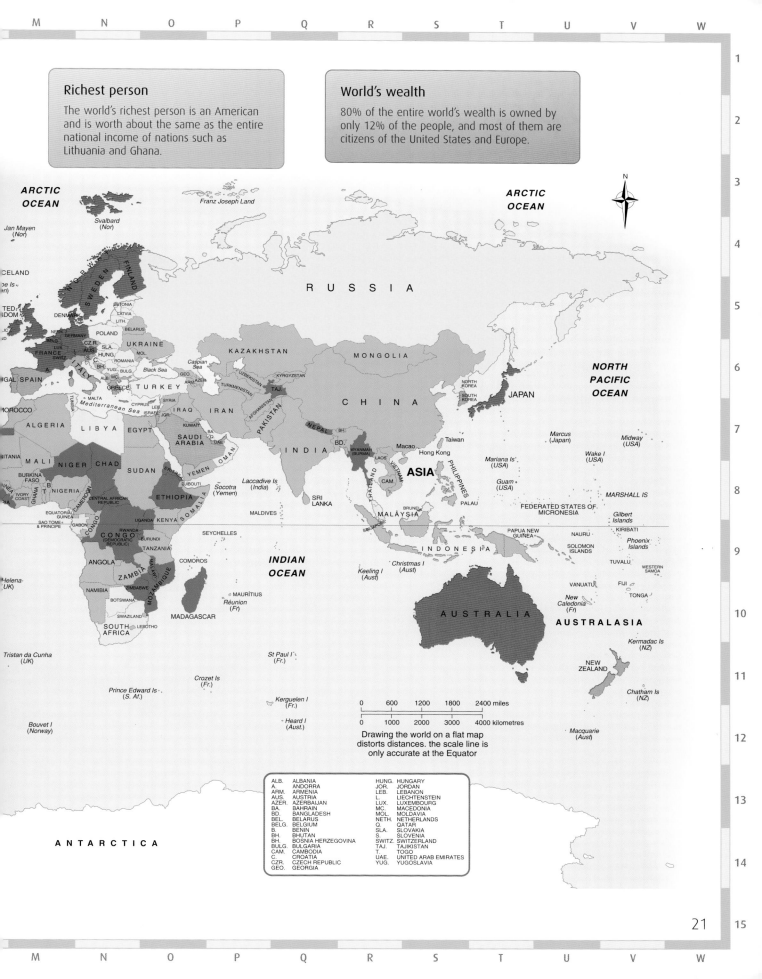

Richest person

The world's richest person is an American and is worth about the same as the entire national income of nations such as Lithuania and Ghana.

World's wealth

80% of the entire world's wealth is owned by only 12% of the people, and most of them are citizens of the United States and Europe.

ARCTIC OCEAN

ARCTIC OCEAN

Jan Mayen (Nor)

Franz Joseph Land

Svalbard (Nor)

N

RUSSIA

ICELAND

NORWAY
SWEDEN
FINLAND

DENMARK

ESTONIA
LATVIA
LITH.
BELARUS

UNITED KINGDOM

NETH.
GERMANY
POLAND
CZ.R.

KAZAKHSTAN

MONGOLIA

NORTH PACIFIC OCEAN

BELG.
LUX.
FRANCE
SWITZ.
AUS.
SLA.
HUNG.
ROMANIA
MOL.
UKRAINE

S.C.
BH.
YUG.
BULG.
ALB.
MC.

Black Sea

GEO.
ARM.
AZER.

UZBEKISTAN
KYRGYZSTAN

NORTH KOREA
SOUTH KOREA

JAPAN

PORTUGAL
SPAIN

ITALY

GREECE
TURKEY

Caspian Sea

TURKMENISTAN
TAJ.

CHINA

Marcus (Japan)

Midway (USA)

MALTA
Mediterranean Sea
TUNISIA

CYPRUS
LEB.
ISRAEL
SYRIA
JOR.

IRAQ

IRAN

AFGHANISTAN

PAKISTAN

NEPAL
BH.

Taiwan

Macao
Hong Kong

Mariana Is (USA)

Wake I (USA)

MOROCCO

ALGERIA

LIBYA

EGYPT

KUWAIT
BA.
QATAR
UAE

SAUDI ARABIA

OMAN

INDIA

BD.

MYANMAH (BURMA)

LAOS
THAILAND
VIETNAM

ASIA

Guam (USA)

MARSHALL IS

MAURITANIA

MALI

NIGER

CHAD

SUDAN

ERITREA
YEMEN

DJIBOUTI

Laccadive Is (India)

CAM.

PHILIPPINES

PALAU

FEDERATED STATES OF MICRONESIA

BURKINA FASO

NIGERIA

ETHIOPIA

Socotra (Yemen)

SRI LANKA

BRUNEI

GUINEA
IVORY COAST
GHANA
B.

EQUATORIAL GUINEA
CAMEROON
CENTRAL AFRICAN REPUBLIC

UGANDA
KENYA
SOMALIA

MALDIVES

MALAYSIA

SINGAPORE

Gilbert Islands

SAO TOME & PRINCIPE
GABON
CONGO

CONGO (DEMOCRATIC REPUBLIC)
RWANDA
BURUNDI

TANZANIA

SEYCHELLES

INDONESIA

PAPUA NEW GUINEA

NAURU

KIRIBATI

SOLOMON ISLANDS

Phoenix Islands

ANGOLA

ZAMBIA
MALAWI
MOZAMBIQUE

COMOROS

INDIAN OCEAN

TUVALU

WESTERN SAMOA

St Helena (UK)

NAMIBIA
ZIMBABWE
BOTSWANA

MAURITIUS
Réunion (Fr)

MADAGASCAR

Christmas I (Aust)

Keeling I (Aust)

VANUATU

FIJI

TONGA

New Caledonia (Fr)

SWAZILAND
SOUTH AFRICA
LESOTHO

AUSTRALIA

AUSTRALASIA

Tristan da Cunha (UK)

St Paul I (Fr.)

Kermadac Is (NZ)

NEW ZEALAND

Chatham Is (NZ)

Prince Edward Is (S. Af.)

Crozet Is (Fr.)

Kerguelen I (Fr.)

| 0 | 600 | 1200 | 1800 | 2400 miles |
| 0 | 1000 | 2000 | 3000 | 4000 kilometres |

Drawing the world on a flat map distorts distances. the scale line is only accurate at the Equator

Bouvet I (Norway)

Heard I (Aust.)

Macquarie (Aust)

ANTARCTICA

ALB.	ALBANIA	HUNG.	HUNGARY
A.	ANDORRA	JOR.	JORDAN
ARM.	ARMENIA	LEB.	LEBANON
AUS.	AUSTRIA	L.	LIECHTENSTEIN
AZER.	AZERBAIJAN	LUX.	LUXEMBOURG
BA.	BAHRAIN	MC.	MACEDONIA
BD.	BANGLADESH	MOL.	MOLDAVIA
BEL.	BELARUS	NETH.	NETHERLANDS
BELG.	BELGIUM	Q.	QATAR
B.	BENIN	SLA.	SLOVAKIA
BH.	BHUTAN	S.	SLOVENIA
BH.	BOSNIA HERZEGOVINA	SWITZ.	SWITZERLAND
BULG.	BULGARIA	TAJ.	TAJIKISTAN
CAM.	CAMBODIA	T.	TOGO
C.	CROATIA	UAE.	UNITED ARAB EMIRATES
CZR.	CZECH REPUBLIC	YUG.	YUGOSLAVIA
GEO.	GEORGIA		

21

Europe

Andorra is a small, landlocked principality on the border between France and Spain. Before the Euro (the common currency for a number of European countries) was launched on 1 January 2002 Andorra did not have a currency, but used the French franc and the Spanish peseta. Andorra is popular with summer and winter tourists – people can go easily to the high peaks in cable cars.

E urope, with its 46 countries, is the second smallest continent but the most heavily populated. It stretches from Iceland, Ireland and Portugal in the Atlantic to the Urals in Russia, and from The Mediterranean in the south to Finland in the North. There are rugged coastlines in the north, hundreds of small islands around Greece and Croatia, and jagged mountains, fens and moorlands in the centre.

A third of the Netherlands is below sea level. This includes the cites of Amsterdam and Rotterdam. For centuries a series of dikes and canals have protected the land from the sea. This will be an increasing problem as sea levels rise due to global warming.

The national borders of Europe have always changed due to the changing political situation. The Countries of former Yugoslavia are still subdividing: in 2006 Montenegro gained independence from Serbia to form Europe's youngest country.

Italy only became unified in 1870: before, it was a series of city-states. Even today, there a two micro states within its borders: San Marino and the Vatican City.

Germany, which was divided after World War II into East and West Germany, was reunited after the fall of Communism in 1990.

Spain was cut off from the rest of Europe for a long time and, until 1492, was ruled by the Moors, an Islamic people from North Africa. Their influence can still be seen in the buildings of Andaluciá.

The country with the world's highest life expectancy is Andorra, with an average age of 83.5 years.

Unlike much of the world, Europe has a declining and ageing population which will create problems in the future, as there won't be so many people in work to support the growing numbers of the elderly.

ICELAND
Reykjavik

NORTH ATLANTIC OCEAN

Faeroe Is (Dmk)

N O R W A Y

S W E D E N

Oslo   Stockholm

North Sea

DENMARK   Copenhagen

UNITED KINGDOM

REPUBLIC OF IRELAND   Dublin

London

NETHER-LANDS   Berlin

Amsterdam   GERMANY   Warsaw

BELGIUM   Brussels   Prague   POLA

LUX.   CZ.R.

Paris   Vienna   Bra

Bern   AUSTRIA   HUNG

FRANCE   SWITZ.   SL.   Zagreb

Ljubljana   CR.

S.M.   BH.

MON.   Sarajevo   MN

AND.   I T A L Y   Crkvice   Tirana

Rome   ALBAN

PORTUGAL   Madrid

Lisbon   SPAIN

Seville   Valetta   MALTA

Gibraltar   M e d i t e r r a

0   300   600   900   1200 miles

0   500   1000   1500   2000 kilometres

The Vatican City, situated within Rome, has the world's smallest population, with just 911 inhabitants.

Monaco is a tiny independent state on the southern coast of Europe, close to the French border with Italy. Its highest point is Le Rocher, only 459 ft (140 m)! It has beautiful beaches, steep cliffs, a mild, sunny climate, and is probably most well-known for the Monaco Grand Prix.

Hot, sunny summers and sandy beaches make the Mediterranean coast one of the world's biggest tourist areas. The Mediterranean Sea is found to the south of Europe and to the north of Africa. It is almost enclosed by land, with just a tiny gap to the south of Spain where it joins the Atlantic Ocean.

ARCTIC OCEAN

FINLAND
● Kuusamo

sinki

Tallinn
STONIA

ATVIA

Vilnius
● Minsk
BELARUS

R U S S I A

■ Moscow

Ust'Shchugor ●

● Kiev

U K R A I N E

Kishinev
MOLDOVIA

ANIA

● Bucharest

GARIA
ofia
e
Black Sea

TURKEY

ens

Nicosia
CYPRUS
te
Sea

AND.	ANDORRA
ARM.	ARMENIA
AZER.	AZERBAIJAN
BH.	BOSNIA HERZEGOVINA
CR.	CROATIA
CZ.R.	CZECH REPUBLIC
GEO.	GEORGIA
L.	LIECHTENSTEIN
LUX.	LUXEMBOURG
MC.	MACEDONIA
MN.	MONTENEGRO
MON.	MONACO
S.M.	SAN MARINO
SL.	SLOVENIA
SLA.	SLOVAKIA
SWITZ.	SWITZERLAND
TAJ.	TAJIKISTAN

DATA BANK

Longest river
Volga (Russia) 2,299 miles (3,700km)

Highest mountain
Mount Elbrus (Russia) 18,510 feet (5,642 m)

Climate
Dry and sunny in the Mediterranean south; snow-covered Alps; mild and damp in Central Europe; occasionally subarctic in northern Norway, Sweden, Finland and Russia.

Natural Resources
Oil, coal, minerals, wind, forest

Population
726,000,000

Richest / poorest country
Luxembourg is the richest country in Europe per head of population and Albania is the poorest

About Europe

The countries of Europe, their capital cities and population:

Country	Capital	Population
Albania	Tirana	3,544,841
Andorra	Andorra la Vella	68,403
Austria	Vienna	8,169,929
Belarus	Minsk	10,335,382
Belgium	Brussels	10,274,595
Bosnia/Herzegovina	Sarajevo	3,964,388
Bulgaria	Sofia	7,421,337
Croatia	Zagreb	4,390,751
Cyprus	Nicosia	767,314
Czech Republic	Prague	10,256,760
Denmark	Copenhagen	7,368,854
Estonia	Tallinn	1,415,681
Finland	Helsinki	5,183,545
France	Paris	60,656,183
Georgia	Tbilisi	4,960,951
Germany	Berlin	83,251,851
Greece	Athens	10,645,343
Hungary	Budapest	10,075,034
Iceland	Reykjavik	279,384
Ireland	Dublin	4,015,676
Italy	Rome	58,103,625
Latvia	Riga	32,842
Liechtenstein	Vaduz	3,601,138
Lithuania	Vilnius	65,200
Luxembourg	Luxembourg	448,569
Macedonia	Skopje	2,054,800
Malta	Valletta	397,499
Moldova	Chisinau	4,434,547
Monaco	Monaco	31,987
Montenegro	Podgorica	620,145
The Netherlands	Amsterdam	16,318,199
Norway	Oslo	4,525,116
Poland	Warsaw	38,625,478
Portugal	Lisbon	10,564,245
Romania	Bucharest	21,698,181
Russian Federation	Moscow	144,978,573
San Marino	San Marino	27,730
Serbia	Belgrade	9,400,000
Slovakia	Bratislava	5,422,366
Slovenia	Ljubljana	1,932,917
Spain	Madrid	40,077,100
Sweden	Stockholm	8,876,744
Switzerland	Berne	7,488,994
Turkey	Ankara	69,660,559
United Kingdom	London	60,441,457
Ukraine	Kiev	48,396,470
Vatican City	Vatican City	911

Famous people

- Anne Frank (1929–45). While hiding from the Nazis during World War II Anne Frank kept a diary of her family's struggles while in hiding in Amsterdam. The family were eventually discovered and sent to a concentration camp at Bergen-Belsen, where she died of typhus. This beautiful rhododendron was named in her memory.

- Alfred Nobel (1833–96) the Swedish inventor of dynamite. In 1900 the Nobel Foundation was set up to fund the annual Peace, Science and Literature prizes.

- Antoni Gaudi (1852–1926) Spain's best known architect. He worked almost exclusively in Barcelona. The 'Sagrada Familia' Church is still not complete, over 100 years after it was started.

- Wolfgang Amadeus Mozart (1756–91) Born in Salzburg, Mozart was one of the most famous composers. He wrote his first symphony aged six and died in Vienna at the age of 35. He is probably most well-known for his operas.

- Mikail Gorbachev (b. 1931) was the last president of the Soviet Union before the collapse of Communism in 1989, and helped bring to an end the Cold War in a peaceful manner.

Land use

- The sunny and dry climate in the south and around the Mediterranean is particularly favourable for grapes and wine-making. Olives grow in abundance, especially in Italy, Greece and Spain.
- Norway has become the wealthiest country in Europe by exploiting the oil and gas resources under the North Sea.
- The plains of central and eastern Europe are largely given over to agriculture.
- The high pastures of the Alpine regions support a thriving dairy industry.

Environment

- The industrial revolution, which originated in northern Europe in the 19th century, produced enormous wealth, and also enormous pollution, because the heavy industries that drove the revolution relied on burning huge quantities of fossil fuels that pumped damaging gases into the atmosphere.
- The challenge of the future is how we maintain our way of life without causing further damage.

- New methods (e.g. wind, wave and solar power) will have to be used far more to generate power as these forms do not pollute the atmosphere. It is possible that nuclear power, currently out of favour because of cost and danger, may be used more in the future.

Industry

- Heavy industry is concentrated in northern Europe specifically in the Ruhr valley in Germany; in the North of England, and also in the Czech Republic and northern Italy. These industries are based around coal, steel and automobile manufacturing. However, they have gone into decline in recent years because of competition from the developing Asian economies and are being replaced by financial and service industries. Electronics are very strong in the Netherlands and Scandinavia.

Recycling household waste

- As Europe has grown wealthier, it has created more and more rubbish, throwing away enormous mountains of waste each year. Treating and disposing of all this material without harming the environment is a major issue.
- Two-thirds of what we throw away is either burnt in incinerators or dumped into landfill sites, but both these methods create environmental damage, are harmful to human health and to plants and animals.
- The trend of producing more and more rubbish has to be reversed. Figures suggest that 60% of all household waste could be recycled or composted, but the largest nation in the UK, England, recycles only 12%.
- We have all seen bottle banks and recycling centres, but the method that makes the biggest improvement is to have different rubbish bins for each type of waste in every household.

Languages

- In spite of its small size Europe has a large number of languages. Apart from the major ones such as English, French, German, Italian, the Slavic languages and Spanish, there are many minority languages eg. Breton in France, Romance in Switzerland and Welsh and Gaelic in the UK, which are all in decline.
- Did you know that 650,000 people use Welsh as their community language?

The British Isles
United Kingdom and Republic of Ireland

The **Republic of Ireland** and the **United Kingdom** together form the British Isles. They form an archipelago (a cluster of islands) off the northwestern coast of Europe. England, Scotland and Wales together form what is known as Great Britain. The United Kingdom covers Great Britain and Northern Ireland. The Republic of Ireland covers approximately 83% of the island of Ireland, and the remaining 17% is known as Northern Ireland, and is part of the United Kingdom.

There are many small islands, most of which belong to the United Kingdom, but some belong neither to the United Kingdom nor the Republic of Ireland. The Isle of Man lies in the Irish Sea between mainland Britain and Ireland, and is a crown dependency, as are the Channel Islands, which lie in the English Channel, very close to the French mainland. Being crown dependencies means that they have their own judicial system (laws) and their own money.

They are not countries in their own right because they are possessions of the British Crown. Three smaller Channel Islands, Alderney, Sark and Herm, are dependencies of Guernsey.

The United Kingdom comprises Great Britain and Northern Ireland. Great Britain is Europe's largest island and for the last 500 years has been one of the world's most influential and richest countries. At its height, the British Empire stretched over 25% of the earth's surface, ruling countries such as Canada, South Africa, India and Australia, which is why so many nations speak English. The Empire is no more, and even Scotland, Wales and Northern Ireland now have their own parliaments. The UK was a world leader in shipbuilding, steel making, car manufacturing and coal mining, but these have declined, with most people now employed in finance, health care, education, retailing and tourism.

Ireland is separated from Great Britain by the Irish Sea, and is known as the Emerald Isle because the mild, wet climate makes the countryside green and attractive. Ireland has a ring of coastal mountains and low central plains. The highest peak is Carrauntuohill, which is 3,414 ft (1,041 m), and the longest river is the Shannon, at 240 miles (386 km). Ireland's economy – nicknamed the 'Celtic Tiger' – has boomed since joining the European Union, and many skilled workers have returned to work in high-technology industries.

Q&A

Q: What is the Giant's Causeway?

A: The Giant's Causeway?(right) is an area of 40,000 interlocking columns resulting from a volcanic eruption over 60 million years ago. It is located along the northeast coast of Ireland.

Q: Why doesn't the Queen rule England?

A: England is ruled by a parliament of elected officials.

Fascinating Facts

The Irish are famous for the art of conversation. Near Cork lies the Blarney Stone, which is said to have the power to make eloquent anyone who kisses it.

Stonehenge (below) is a monument of huge stones located in the English county of Wiltshire. It is one of the most famous prehistoric sites in the world. Archaeologists think the standing stones were erected between 2500 and 2000 BC.

Britain is home to the world's most poisonous fungus; the yellowish-olive Death Cap.

DATA BANK

Longest river
Shannon (Ireland) 240 miles (386 km)

Highest mountain
Ben Nevis (Scotland) 4,406 ft (1,343 m)

Coastline
8,618 miles (13, 870 km)

Climate
More than 195 inches (500 cm) of rain in the higher regions and less than 20 inches (50 cm) in the lowlands. Mild winters with a little snow, cool summers

Largest city and population
London (England) 7,465,100

Annual income
US $35,000 or £20,000 approx. per person

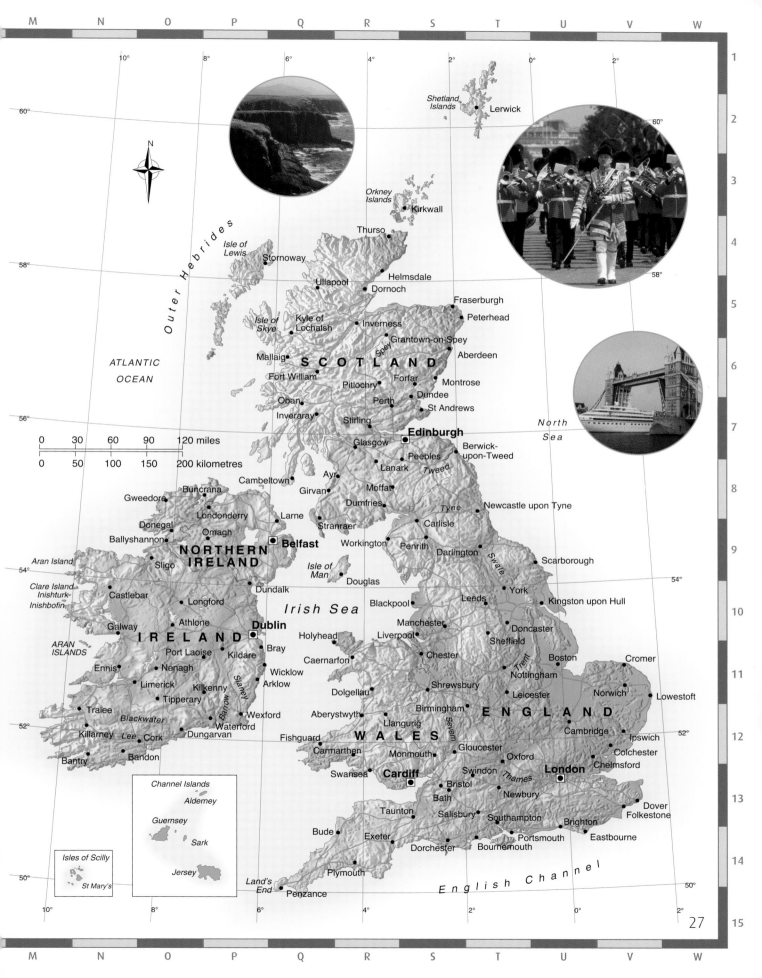

About the British Isles

The countries of The British Isles, their capital cities and population:

England	London	49,138,831
Ireland	Dublin	4,015,676
Northern Ireland	Belfast	1,685,267
Scotland	Edinburgh	5,062,011
Wales	Cardiff	2,903,085

Languages

Predominantly English. Welsh is spoken by 25% of the Welsh people and Gaelic is spoken to a lesser extent in Western Scotland and the Hebrides. Irish is spoken by approximately 25% of the population. Cornish is spoken in small areas of Cornwall.

The UK is a multicultural society and many languages are spoken, mainly from the Indian sub continent and Africa.

Famous people

- William Shakespeare (1546–1616) Born in Stratford-upon-Avon, England. Dramatist of towering stature and whose worldwide fame supports a huge part of the UK's tourist industry.

- Robert Burns (1759–1796) Scotland's national poet (below). The Scots remember him with unique affection. 'When Scotland forgets Burns, then history will forget Scotland' (J S Blackie 19th century Scottish educationalist). *Auld Lang Syne* is sung the world over on New Year's Day.

- Mary Robinson (b. 1944) First woman president of the Republic of Ireland 1990–1997 and United Commissioner for Human Rights 1997–2002. She was credited with liberalising the very conservative office of the Irish Presidency.

- James Joyce (1882-1941) Irish-born writer and novelist, best known for *The Dubliners* and *Finnegan's Wake*

- Dylan Thomas, (1924-1953) Born in Swansea. During his lifetime he wrote many great poems, and the 'play for voices,' *Under Milk Wood*. He did most of his writing in his 'work-shed' (below).

Land use

- The Industrial Revolution started in the UK in the early 19th century. The introduction of major mills and factories instead of cottage industries caused a mass migration away from the countryside to the booming new northern cities.

- New machinery was also introduced onto the farms, which had a profound effect on land use. Threshing machines took over from individuals harvesting by hand. They even separated the seeds from the heads and stalks. Steam-powered tractors became the new source of energy in place of horses.

- Heavy industry was concentrated in the northern cities from Liverpool to Leeds, Glasgow in Scotland, and the South Wales valleys.

- Until very recently Ireland had always been poor and relied on the potato harvest, which catastrophically failed in the 1840s, causing mass migrations to the UK and the USA. Today it is a booming economy of the EU.

Industry

- During the 19th and early 20th centuries the UK became a great manufacturing power and a pioneer in new transport systems – the railway and motor car. Heavy industry is concentrated in the northern cities such as Liverpool, Birmingham and Leeds, and around Glasgow in Scotland, and the South Wales valleys.

- Today, machine tools, electric power equipment, automation equipment, railroad equipment, aircraft, motor vehicles and parts, electronics and communications equipment, metals, chemicals, coal, petroleum, paper and paper products, food processing, textiles, clothing and other consumer goods make up the industries found in the United Kingdom and in Ireland.

Natural resources

- Coal: very little coal is mined, although there are massive untapped reserves.
- Oil and gas: these are found in the North Sea but are rapidly declining.
- Wind: many wind farms are now being built in an attempt to find more environmentally friendly ways of generating power.

Environment

- The scars of the first industrial revolution are being healed. The coal tips of South Wales have been cleared and planted over. The Clean Air Act of the 1950s, when it became compulsory to burn smokeless coal, actually changed the weather, and industrial smog became a thing of the past.

England

- England is the largest of the British nations and has, in London, one of the most cosmopolitan capital cities in the world. It is home to both the government and the monarchy, and the headquarters of many national institutions and companies. This combination of royalty and national monuments attracts tourists from around the world. The most visited sights are Westminster Abbey, Downing Street and St Paul's Cathedral (below).

Ireland

- The River Shannon is Ireland's longest river; it is 161 miles (259 km) long and flows south and west from County Cavan and through the Shannon Estuary before emptying into the Atlantic Ocean.
- Dublin, the capital, a city of fine Georgian squares, is at the mouth of the Liffey River where it enters the Irish Sea. Over 25% of Ireland's population live in Dublin, the centre of government, finance, education and the new, high-technology industries, as well as brewing and tourism.
- The shamrock, a symbol for Ireland, is a three-leafed young white clover, often used as a badge for sports teams and state occasions.

Wales

- Successive English kings tried to integrate Wales into England. King Edward I ordered a ring of castles to be built to circle the land, but it was not until the reign of Henry VIII that Wales was fully under control. The castles today remain as magnificent tourist attractions.

- Wales is a rugged country. In the north are the magnificent mountains of Snowdonia. Mid-Wales has a more rolling countryside, but is very sparsely populated, while in the south are the Black Mountains and the coal-rich Welsh valleys. It is in this region that the capital, Cardiff is situated and where most of the people live.

Scotland

- The Celts of Scotland have always fiercely defended their homeland. The Romans could not defeat them and built two walls, The Antonine Wall (between the River Clyde and the Firth of Forth) and Hadrian's Wall (between the River Solway and River Tyne), to try and keep them out. England and Scotland became unified in 1707.

- The Scots achieved their own parliament in 1998, with elected representatives who have total control over issues such as education, health, agriculture, and justice. The parliament is in the capital city of Edinburgh, which has many fine buildings such as Edinburgh Castle and Holyrood House.

Northern Ireland

- Northern Ireland consists of the six counties of Ulster and is situated in the northeast of Ireland. It covers 5,459 sq miles (14,139 sq km), about a sixth of the total area of the island. It is mostly rural, with industry centred around the capital Belfast.
- Lough Neagh is the largest freshwater lake in the British Isles, and the third largest lake in Western Europe. It is approximately 20 miles (30 km) long and 9 miles (15 km) wide. The lake is very shallow around the margins and has an average depth of about 30 feet (9 m), although at its deepest it is about 80 feet (25 m) deep.

Scandinavia

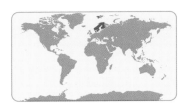

The countries of Norway, Sweden, Denmark and Finland are known as Scandinavia, and are Europe's most northerly and least populated. They stretch from Norway's mountainous Atlantic coast in the west, to Finland's northerly low-lying, forested countryside. More than a third of Finland lies within the Arctic Circle where, during the 73-day summer period of the Midnight Sun, darkness never completely falls. In the north, temperatures fall below –20°F (–29°C) in winter and rise to more than 80°F (27°C) in summer. Denmark also rules Greenland.

Sweden

Sweden's high standard of living is due to a mixed system of high-tech capitalism and extensive welfare benefits. Sweden and Finland followed Denmark, a long-established member, in joining the EU in 1995, whilst Norway remains outside.

Norway

Since Norway's traditional industries of fishing, timber and manufacturing have declined, the country has become dependent on its vast North Sea oil and gas fields for its prosperity. The North Cape of Norway is over 994 miles (1,600 km) within the Arctic Circle. It has deep inlets, called fjords, that reach into the rugged interior with its snow-capped mountains. The sun does not set for a period of about 10 weeks, from mid-May to the end of July.

Denmark

Denmark was home to the seafaring Vikings who controlled and settled much of Northern Europe. Vikings reached North America over 1,000 years ago. Denmark is the southernmost and smallest of the Scandinavian countries, occupying the Jutland Peninsula and over 450 small islands. Copenhagen, the capital, is an attractive city with an old town district, the Tivoli Gardens, and a famous statue of the Little Mermaid in the harbour (below).

Q&A

Q: Are there reindeer in Scandinavia?

A: Yes. The northern areas of Norway, Sweden and Finland are known as Lapland, and reindeer (left) are found here, particularly in northern Norway. The native people of northern Norway, known as the Sami, still herd reindeer.

Q: Can you really drive across the sea from Denmark to Sweden?

A: Yes, but you have to travel under the sea as well, by tunnel from Copenhagen, and then across the Øresund Bridge to Malmö in Sweden. There is also a railway line.

Finland

Finland's capital is Helsinki. Lapland, in northern Finland, is said to be where Father Christmas lives. Just before Christmas many tourists fly to Lapland to meet him and have fun in the snow.

DATA BANK

Longest river
Klara-Göta (Sweden) 447 miles (720 km)

Highest mountain
Galdhøpiggen (Norway) 8,100 ft (2,469 m)

Coastline
20,945 miles (33,707 km)

Climate
Norway's mountains have more than 195 inches (500 cm) of rain but less than 20 inches (50 cm) falls in east Finland. Cool, sunny summers and very cold winters with several months of snow.

Largest city and population
Stockholm (Sweden) 1,622,300

Annual income
US $30,000 or £17,000 approx. per person

Fascinating Facts

Finland has more lakes than any other country. Its 187,888 lakes cover 10% of the country.

Oslo is the world's most expensive city.

The Ice Hotel in Jukkasjärvi, Sweden, is rebuilt every December and has 80 double rooms and an interior temperature of 22°F (–6°C).

M N O P Q R S T U V W

1

2

BARENTS SEA

Nordkapp
Kjelvik
Berlevåg
Hammerfest
Lebesby
Hamningberg
Vadsø
Alta
Kirkenes

NORWEGIAN SEA

Tromsø
Karasjok
Utsjoki

VESTERÅLEN

Lenvik
Målselv
Enontekiö

Hadsel
Narvik
Kiruna
Kittilä
Sodankylä

Svolvær
Vittangi

LOFOTEN

Sørfold
Gällivare
Rovaniemi

Bodø

Saltdal
Jokkmokk

Arctic Circle

Mo i Rana
Tornio
Kemi

Mosjøen
Boden
Luleå

Brønnøysund
Sorsele
Skellefteälv
Hailuoto
Oulu

Storuman
Raahe
Vuokatti

Namsos
Grong
Vilhelmina
Lycksele
FINLAND
Iisalmi

Umeälv
Jakobstad
Kuopio

Hoting
Umeå
Varkaus

Stjørdal
Hotagen
Lapua

Kristiansund
SWEDEN
Kramfors
Kaskinen

Trondheim
Sundsvall

Ålesund

NORWAY
Linsell
Hudiksvall
Pori
Tampere
Sysma

Norddal
Dombås
Lillhärdal
Söderhamn
Rauma

▲ *Galdhøpiggen*
8,100 ft
2,469 m
Los

Lillehammer
Rättvik
Gävle
Helsinki

Bergen
Hamar
ÅLAND
Naantali

Myrdal
Borlänge
Hangö

Uskedal
Drammen
Oslo
Västerdalälven
Uppsala

Haugesund
Dalen
Karlstad
Örebro
Stockholm

Stavanger
Larvik
Strömstad
Vänern

Egersund
Evje
Arendal
Norrköping

Mandal
Kristiansand
Skagerrak
Trollhättan
Linköping
GOTLAND

Hjørring
Göteborg
Huskvarna
Visby

Ålborg
Vetlanda
Målilla
BALTIC SEA

Ringkøbing
Viborg
Kattegat
Varberg
Borgholm

Halmstad
ÖLAND

DENMARK
Horsens
Helsingborg
Karlskrona

Copenhagen
Kristianstad

Esbjerg
Malmö

Odense
Bornholm

NORTH SEA

0   50   100   150   200 miles

0   100   200   300   400 kilometres

M N O P Q R S T U V W

Low Countries

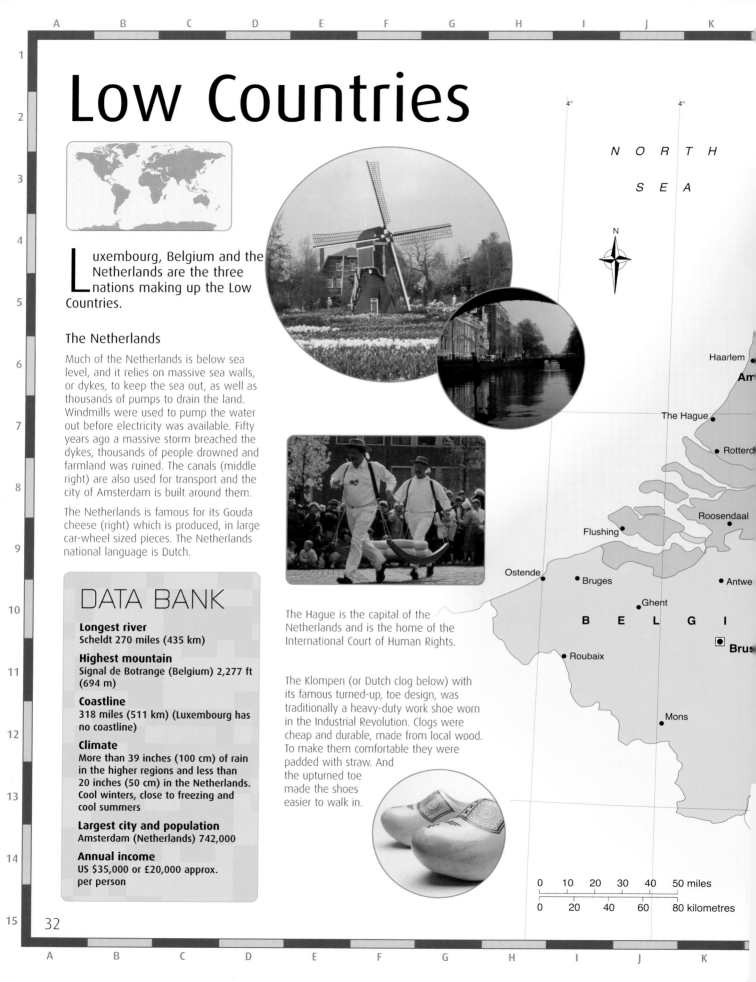

Luxembourg, Belgium and the Netherlands are the three nations making up the Low Countries.

The Netherlands

Much of the Netherlands is below sea level, and it relies on massive sea walls, or dykes, to keep the sea out, as well as thousands of pumps to drain the land. Windmills were used to pump the water out before electricity was available. Fifty years ago a massive storm breached the dykes, thousands of people drowned and farmland was ruined. The canals (middle right) are also used for transport and the city of Amsterdam is built around them.

The Netherlands is famous for its Gouda cheese (right) which is produced, in large car-wheel sized pieces. The Netherlands national language is Dutch.

DATA BANK

Longest river
Scheldt 270 miles (435 km)

Highest mountain
Signal de Botrange (Belgium) 2,277 ft (694 m)

Coastline
318 miles (511 km) (Luxembourg has no coastline)

Climate
More than 39 inches (100 cm) of rain in the higher regions and less than 20 inches (50 cm) in the Netherlands. Cool winters, close to freezing and cool summers

Largest city and population
Amsterdam (Netherlands) 742,000

Annual income
US $35,000 or £20,000 approx. per person

The Hague is the capital of the Netherlands and is the home of the International Court of Human Rights.

The Klompen (or Dutch clog below) with its famous turned-up, toe design, was traditionally a heavy-duty work shoe worn in the Industrial Revolution. Clogs were cheap and durable, made from local wood. To make them comfortable they were padded with straw. And the upturned toe made the shoes easier to walk in.

NORTH SEA

N

Haarlem
Am
The Hague
Rotterd
Roosendaal
Flushing
Ostende
Bruges
Antwe
Ghent
B E L G I
Brus
Roubaix
Mons

0 10 20 30 40 50 miles

0 20 40 60 80 kilometres

6°   7°

Islands

• Harlingen

Groningen •

• Heerenveen

Emmen •

• Zwelle

Enschede •

ERLANDS

52°

Utrecht

Rhine   • Arnhem

Meuse

Nijmegen •

Tilburg

• Eindhoven

Maastricht •

• Liege

▲
Signal de
Botrange
2,277 ft
694 m

50°

Neufchateau •

LUXEMBOURG

▣ **Luxembourg**

Fascinating Facts

The Oosterscheldedam, in the southwest of the Netherlands, is the world's largest tidal river barrier, with a total length of 5.5 miles (9 km).

Despite there being no diamond mines in Europe, Antwerp is the world centre of the diamond cutting industry, producing fine quality diamonds for jewellery and industry.

Tulips (left) originally come from Turkey, but have been grown in the Netherlands for over 450 years.

Belgium

Brussels is the capital of Belgium, and is also the headquarters of the European Union and NATO. Three languages are spoken here – Dutch and French, and in the northern region called Flanders the language is called Flemish.

Belgian chocolates are world famous for their quality and tasty fillings, such as praline.

Luxembourg

Luxembourg city is the capital of Luxembourg and is a major banking centre. Although it is a small country, it has 12 cities. The citizens often travel into neighbouring countries to work, most people speak three languages – Dutch, French and German. The language of Luxembourg itself is called Luxembourgish.

Q&A

Q: Why is the Netherlands sometimes called Holland?

A: The Netherlands and Holland are often used to describe the same country, but Holland is an area of the Netherlands. Holland is in fact the most densely populated area of the Netherlands, where there are a lot of major cities

Q: Why is Luxembourg called the Grand Duchy of Luxembourg?

A: A grand duchy is a territory whose head of state is a Grand Duke or Grand Duchess; Luxembourg is a parliamentary democracy ruled by a Grand Duke.

33

France

France is the third largest country in Europe, and has the fourth highest population. Despite having a rural landscape, over 70% of the population live in the cities, with more than 16% in the greater Paris area.

France has an excellent health, educational and social care system and is the fifth most wealthy country in the world. Northern France is industrialised, low-lying and cool, but, in the south, the snow-capped peaks of the Alps and Pyrenées are close to the warm and sunny beaches of the Mediterranean Sea.

France invests much money in excellent motorways and railways. Rail travel is cheap and the 186 mph (300 km/h) *Train Grande Vitesse* (TGV) connects all the major cities. There are also rail links to London and many other countries.

DATA BANK

Longest river
Loire 628 miles (1,010 km)

Highest mountain
Mont Blanc 15,771 ft (4,807 m)

Coastline
3,418 miles (5,500 km)

Climate
From more than 98 inches (250 cm) of rain and snow in the Alps, to less than 20 inches (50 cm) on the Mediterranean coast near Spain. There is permanent snow in the Alps but less than one day of frost per year on the Mediterranean coast.

Largest city and population
Paris 2,113,000

Annual income
US $28,700 or £16,000 approx. per person

Almost 80% of France's electricity is generated by nuclear power, and so the French people are less worried about high oil costs than almost any other European country. In mountainous areas, electricity is generated by hydroelectric power stations.

The Eiffel Tower (far right) is the most famous landmark and tourist attraction in Paris. It was built in 1889 for the Great Exhibition and originally was only meant to be a temporary structure. It is named after it's architect, Gustave Eiffel. It is by far the highest structure in Paris 986 ft (300 m) excluding the radio antenna, which was added later. Until 1930 it was the tallest structure in the world until it was overtaken by the Chrysler Building in New York, USA. Every seven years it has to be re-painted with three coats of paint to protect it from rust, which adds 50 tonnes to its weight. The final coat is changed each time. At present it is a shade of brown.

The Arc de Triomphe is another very distinctive landmark in Paris. It copies the style that the Romans used to commemorate their military conquests, but is larger than anything that the Romans built. It was planned in 1806 to commemorate Napolean Bonaparte's victory at Austerlitz, but was not completed until 1836. In the early days of flying, a dare-devil flew his aeroplane through it!

In the 20th century many modern landmarks were built in Paris, the most famous being the glass pyramid at the entrance to the Louvre (left), and the Pompidou Centre.

Calais
oulogne
Lille
Amiens
Rouen
Seine
Paris
Reims
Metz
Nancy
Strasbourg
Troyes
Mulhouse
Orléans
ans
Dijon
Besançon
Bourges
Loire
R A N C E
noges
Clermont-Ferrand
Lyon
Mont Blanc
15,771 ft
4,807 m
Brive
St.-Étienne
Grenoble
Central Massif
Rhône
A l p s
Nîmes
Avignon
Montpellier
Nice
Cannes
use
Marseille
Toulon
Perpignan
M e d i t e r r a n e a n   S e a

Bastia
Corsica
Ajaccio
Bonifacio

N
50°
48°
46°
44°
42°
2° 4° 6° 8° 10°

Q&A

Q: Why is France the world's most visited tourist destination with 75 million visitors a year?

A: Film stars flock to Cannes each spring; millions go skiing in the winter to places like Chamonix, and take beach holidays in summer. The great cities, monuments and scenery attract visitors all the year round.

Q: Has France always been one of the world's most powerful and wealthy countries?

A: Yes, for the last 1,000 years. The Romans built roads, cities and aqueducts, such as Pont Du Gard (left), and in the Middle Ages, rich landowners and aristocrats built many grand chateaux.

Fascinating Facts

Every summer more than 100 professional cyclists race in the Tour de France. The race is approximately 2,480 miles (4,000 km) long. Lasting up to three weeks, the race is held in July.

Under half of French people bathe or shower every day, but French men and women buy more beauty products than any other people on earth.

A total of 270 million trees were destroyed by a storm that hit France on December 26 and 27, 1999. The storm lasted 30 hours, causing 87 deaths.

France is known the world over for its fine wines, and by value it produces more wine than any other nation, though the Italians produce more in quantity and the Spanish have more land under vineyards.

Different types of wine are grown in different areas of France according to the soil type and climate. Some of the well-known names are Champagne, Bordeaux and Burgundy.

France did not export wine until after 1830, but it was only after 1945, when transport links really improved, that the French themselves started appreciating wines made outside their own locale. Before that they had only drunk their local wine.

Germany

A major industrialised nation, Germany is home to the world's third largest economy, after the United States and Japan.

Germany is a leading producer of products such as iron and steel, machinery and machine tools, and automobiles. The famous and luxurious cars of BMW, Mercedes and Porsche are all German makes.

The world's first motorway was built in Berlin between 1913 and 1921. By the end of World War II, the Autobahn network totalled 1,322 miles (2,128 km). There are now over 7,456 miles (12,000 km) of motorway making the Autobahn network the world's second largest superhighway system after the United States' Interstate system.

DATA BANK

Longest river
Rhine 820 miles (1,319 km)

Highest mountain
Zugspitze 9,718 ft (2,962 m)

Coastline
1,484 miles (2,389 km)

Climate
From more than 78 inches (200 cm) of rain and snow in the Alps, to less than 20 inches (50 cm) on the northern Baltic Sea coast. The Bavarian Alps have very snowy winters. Most areas have winters just above freezing and cool summers.

Largest city and population
Berlin 3,426,000

Annual income
US $28,700 or £16,500 approx. per person

Fascinating Facts

Oktoberfest is a two-week festival of eating and drinking held each year in Munich since October 1810. There are 1,250 breweries in Germany. Becks produced the most beer in 2002, with an unbelievable 551 billion litres.

In Germany you can buy more than 300 sorts of bread and more than 1,500 types of sausages and cold meats.

Germans are the world champions in paper recycling, reusing over 75% of all paper consumed.

Berlin, Europe's second largest city, is the capital of Germany (below). It is situated on the banks of the River Spree in the northeast of the country. The city attracts visitors of all ages with its world-class museums, its new art scene and music clubs. Children especially like the city's beautiful parks and its two famous zoos. Each year since the early 1990s, the Love Parade, the world's biggest techno rave, has streamed through Berlin, bringing more than one million young people from all over the globe to each gathering.

Flensburg

chleswig

Rendsburg

Heide

Kiel

Fehmarn

Burg

Sassnitz

Rügen

Stralsund

Rostock

ven

Lübeck

Anklam

Güstrow

Hamburg

Parchim

Bucholz

Neustrelitz

Prenzlau

en

Elbe

Wittenberge

Salzwedel

Aller

Wolfsburg

Brandenburg

Oder

Berlin

Frankfurt
(an der Oder)

Hannover

Potsdam

eser

Magdeburg

Bad Harzburg

Wittenberg

Lübben

Osterode

Bernberg

Elbe

Cottbus

G E R M A N Y

Halle

Mühlhausen

Leipzig

Meissen

Görlitz

Erfurt

Dresden

Eisenach

Jena

Freiberg

eld

Fulda

Werrer

Zwickau

Coburg

Main

Würzburg

Bamberg

Bayreuth

ain

Ansbach

Nürnberg

Regensburg

uttgart

Donauwörth

Ingolstadt

Heidenheim

Danube

Passau

tlingen

Landshut

Ulm

Augsburg

Inn

Munich

ngarten

Rosenheim

B a v a r i a n   A l p s

▲ Zugspitze
9,718 ft
2,962 m

| 0 | 30 | 60 | 90 | 120 miles |

| 0 | 50 | 100 | 150 | 200 kilometres |

After World War II Germany was split into West Germany and East Germany. Many East Germans moved to the West where life was freer and richer. In 1961 the East surrounded West Berlin with a concrete wall, 13 ft (4 m) high and 103 miles (166 km) long (above). At least 170 people died trying to cross the border. East Germany reunited with West Germany in 1990 and the wall was removed.

The Berlin Wall is now commemorated by a few remaining sections and by a museum and shop near the site of the most famous crossing point, Checkpoint Charlie.

Q&A

Q: Why do German children go to school on Saturday mornings?

A: Their normal school day starts at about 8:00 a.m., and ends around 2:00 p.m. so Saturday morning school makes up for the shorter days.

Q: Where do Germans go for beach holidays?

A: Hitting the beach in Germany generally means heading for the North Sea or Baltic Sea coasts. Most Germans head south to France or Spain where there are warmer, sunnier beaches.

37

Austria

L andlocked in Central Europe, Austria has extraordinary Alpine scenery and cultural attractions which have transformed it into a major tourist destination.

Perhaps no one country can match the musical history of Austria, which is the homeland of such legendary composers as Brahms, Haydn, Mahler, Mozart, Schubert and the Strausses. The German-born Ludwig van Beethoven also lived in Vienna for most of his adult life. Combined with an abundance of natural beauty, spectacular mountain vistas and world class Alpine skiing, Austria is an attractive tourist destination. Most industry is in the east, near the Slovakian border, away from the scenic areas.

DATA BANK

Longest river
Danube 1,771 miles (2,850 km)

Highest mountain
Grossglockner 12,461 ft (3,798 m)

Coastline
Austria has no coastline

Climate
From more than 78 inches (200 cm) of rain and snow in the Alps to less than 32 inches (80 cm) on the eastern border with Hungary. There is permanent snow in the Alps and winters are cold everywhere, with a warm summer in the lowlands.

Largest city and population
Vienna 1,543,100

Annual income
US $27,700 or £16,000 approx. per person

10°   11°   12°   13

0	20	40	60 miles

0	20	40	60	80	100 kilometres

48°

● Bregenz
● Dornbirn

Inn

● Kitzbühel

Innsbruck ●

A u s t r i a n   A l p

42°

Wild Spitze
12,217 ft
3,724 m ▲

Grossvenediger
11,978 ft
3,651 m ▲

Grossgl
▲ *12,461 f*
3,798 m

● Lienz

10°   11°   12°   13°

Austria has a small population with a work force of only around 4,000,000 people. The main industries, construction machinery, vehicle parts, iron and steel, chemicals and communications equipment, are found in the east of the country near the border with Slovakia. The capital city, Vienna is a popular tourist site – its new, modern architecture sits happily alongside the medieval buildings that people flock to see. In the more mountainous regions of central and western Austria the industries are food, timber and tourism.

Vienna is the capital of Austria and is situated in the far east of the country. It is at the heart of Europe, smack on the intersection between the East and West. Conquerors such as Celts, Romans, and finally the Habsburgs, have all left their mark. Vienna is enchanting. From the ornate facades of the old state palaces (left) to the horses and carriages (right) that carry tourists past the oak-panelled coffee houses with their delicious coffee and cakes, the city has some of the world's finest art collections, orchestras and opera houses.

Q&A

Q: Which Austrian town has hosted two Olympic Games?

A: Innsbruck in western Austria, is an internationally renowned winter sports centre. Skiing is possible even in the summer on nearby glaciers. The Winter Olympics have been held in Innsbruck twice, first in 1964, then in 1976.

Q: Which country has the greatest percentage of organic farms?

A: Austria has over 10% of its land farmed organically, with more than 20,000 organic farms in operation.

14°   15°   16°   17°

N

Linz

Krems

Danube

Floridsorf

St. Polten

Vienna

Steyr

48°

Wiener Neustadt

U S T R I A

Kapfenberg

Graz

42°

ch

Klagenfurt

14°

Fascinating Facts

The Café Tomaselli in Salzburg has been serving coffee and cakes since 1705, and the composer Mozart was a regular.

Perhaps the most unusual Austrian festival is Perchtenlaufen, held every January in Salzburgerland (below left). The highlight is a street procession with men wearing heavy ornamental headdresses.

The world's largest accessible ice caves are in the mountains near Salzburg.

A world record total of 240 people died and over 45,000 were trapped on January 20, 1951 when a series of avalanches hit the Austrian Alps.

Switzerland

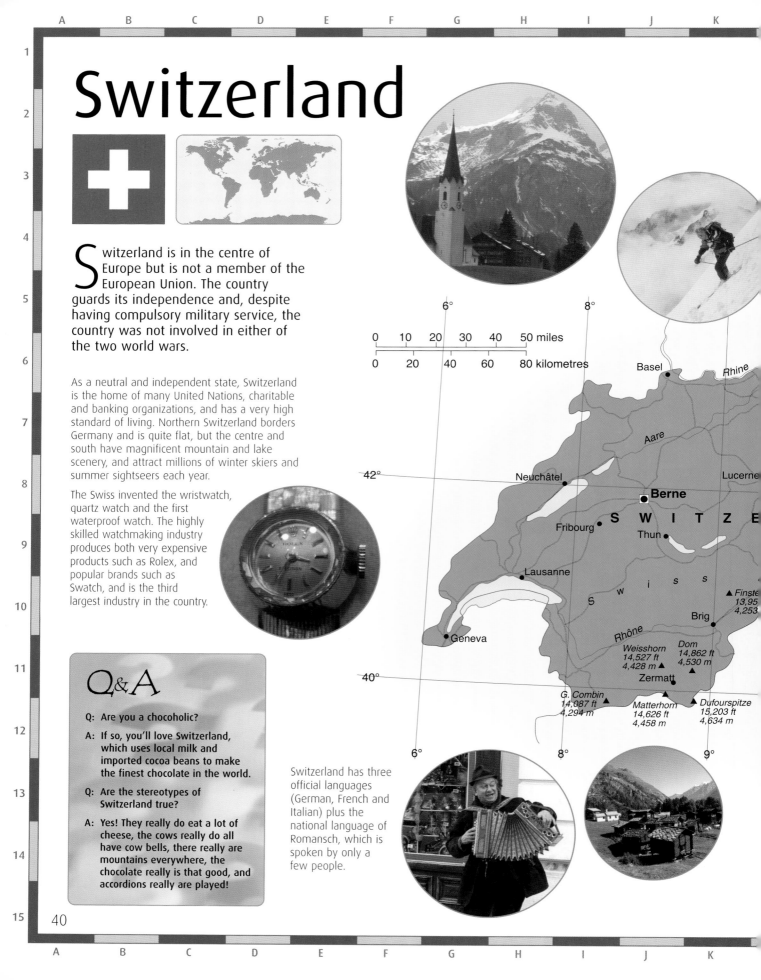

S witzerland is in the centre of Europe but is not a member of the European Union. The country guards its independence and, despite having compulsory military service, the country was not involved in either of the two world wars.

As a neutral and independent state, Switzerland is the home of many United Nations, charitable and banking organizations, and has a very high standard of living. Northern Switzerland borders Germany and is quite flat, but the centre and south have magnificent mountain and lake scenery, and attract millions of winter skiers and summer sightseers each year.

The Swiss invented the wristwatch, quartz watch and the first waterproof watch. The highly skilled watchmaking industry produces both very expensive products such as Rolex, and popular brands such as Swatch, and is the third largest industry in the country.

Q&A

Q: Are you a chocoholic?

A: If so, you'll love Switzerland, which uses local milk and imported cocoa beans to make the finest chocolate in the world.

Q: Are the stereotypes of Switzerland true?

A: Yes! They really do eat a lot of cheese, the cows really do all have cow bells, there really are mountains everywhere, the chocolate really is that good, and accordions really are played!

0 10 20 30 40 50 miles

0 20 40 60 80 kilometres

Basel
Rhine
Aare
42°
Neuchâtel
Lucerne
Berne
Fribourg S W I T Z E
Thun
Lausanne
S w i s s
▲ Finste
13,95
4,253
Brig
Rhône
Geneva
Weisshorn
14,527 ft
4,428 m ▲
Dom
14,862 ft
4,530 m
40°
Zermatt
G. Combin
14,087 ft
4,294 m ▲
Matterhorn
14,626 ft
4,458 m ▲
Dufourspitze
15,203 ft
4,634 m ▲
6° 8° 9°
6° 8°

Switzerland has three official languages (German, French and Italian) plus the national language of Romansch, which is spoken by only a few people.

Berne is the capital of Switzerland. Berne is located in central Switzerland, 122 km from Zurich, on the banks of the River Aare (left). The River is so clean that in summer locals swim and cool off in the middle of town. This is the city where Albert Einstein worked, the Toblerone chocolate bar is made, and Emmental cheese manufactured.

Fascinating Facts

Fondue is a classic Swiss meal made of bread dunked in melted Emmental and Gruyère cheeses (left) mixed with white wine and flour.

Switzerland may be cloudy, but it has the highest use of solar energy in the world.

Every Swiss home has an underground nuclear shelter complete with enough food for one year.

Swiss railways are the most punctual in the world, and special trains climb mountain slopes and even tunnel through rock to reach the summit of the Jungfrau mountain (below).

10° 11° N 42° 40° 10°

Winterthur
St Gallen
rich
ng
L A N D
Rhine
Chur
Davos
p s
St. Moritz
Bellinzona
Lugano
Arosa

DATA BANK

Longest river
Rhine 820 miles (1,319 km)

Highest mountain
Dufourspitze 15,203 ft (4,634 m)

Coastline
Switzerland has no coastline

Climate
Varies by altitude from more than 98 inches (250 cm) of rain and snow in the Alps, to less than 30 inches (75 cm) on the northern border with Germany. There is permanent snow in the Alps and winters are cold everywhere, with a warm summer in the northern lowlands.

Largest city and population
Zurich 333,400

Annual income
US $33,800 or £19,000 approx. per person

Italy

Italy, or the Italian Republic, is in Southern Europe. It shares its northern border with France, Switzerland, Austria and Slovenia, and has two large islands called Sicily and Sardinia. Shaped rather like a boot, Italy is a peninsula – this means that most of the land is surrounded by sea. The independent nation of San Marino can be found towards the right-hand side of this peninsula just above the "knee" of the boot.

Modern Italy has the Alps in the north, forming a natural border with France, Switzerland and Austria, and mountains run the length of Italy all the way to Sicily.

Northern Italy is wealthy, making many famous goods such as Ferrari cars (above) and Armani clothes, whilst the south is mainly agricultural and much poorer.

Rome, the capital city of Italy, is also the site of the Vatican City, which is the smallest independent nation in the world. It is governed by the head of the Roman Catholic Church, the Pope. As well as being the seat of Italy's government, Rome is one of the world's major tourist venues, with people visiting the sights of ancient Rome, such as the Colosseum (where the gladiators fought), St Peter's Basilica (below), and fantastic public buildings, shops and museums.

DATA BANK

Longest river
Po 405 miles (652 km)

Highest mountain
Monte Bianco de Courmayeur 15,577 ft (4,748 m)

Coastline
4,722 miles (7,600 km)

Climate
The wettest areas are in the Alps and the driest are in the south. Permanent snow in the Alps to hot summers in the south with no winter frost by the Mediterranean Sea

Largest city and population
Rome 2,649,500

Annual income
US $27,700 or £16,000 approx. per person

1

12°   14°   16°   18°

N

·no
· Pieve di
  Cadore
· Borgo   Udine ·
Treviso ·   Trieste ·
· Vicenza
Padova · · Venice
· Ferrara · Chioggia
Reno · Porto Tolle
· Ravenna
ogna · Rimini   SAN MARINO
        · Pesaro
rence
·ezzo · Ancona
      · Osimo
· Perugia   · San Benedetto
I T A L Y
·sseto · Terni · Norcia · Teramo
·   · Rieti *Tevere*
·chia   · Pescara
· Rome   · Vasto   · Peschici
ITY · Avezzan   · Termoli   · Vieste
      · Latina   · Foggia
        · Isernia
        · Benevento   *Ofanto*   · Bari
        · Naples   · Melfi
· I. d'Ischia   · Potenza   · Brindisi
      · Salerno   · Taranto
        · Agropoli   · Gallipoli
          · Senise   · Tricase
        · Scalea   · Castrovilla
            · Rossano
          · Cosenza
        · Amantea   · Crotone
    ISOLE   *I. Stromboli*
  EOLIE O LIPARI
    I. Salina   · Vibo Valentia
      I. Lipari
    I. Vulcano   · Palmi
· Trapani · Palermo · Messina
    · Alcamo   · Reggio
Isole Egadi
· Mazara   *S i c i l y*
del Vallo   · Caltanissetta   · Catania
  · Agrigento
          · Siracusa
      · Ragusa

42°

40°

12°   14°   16°   18°

Fascinating Facts

Many famous artists have lived in Italy, including sculptor and painter Michelangelo, and Leonardo da Vinci, who is especially known for the 'Mona Lisa' (left), his painting which hangs in the Louvre museum in Paris.

Italian cooking is world famous. Pasta and pizza are popular worldwide. The biggest pizza ever made measured 122 ft (37.4 m) in diameter

The gondola (left), a rowing craft used in Venice, Italy has a slight curve along its centre line, making up for the fact that it is rowed by one oarsman, and so the boat travels in a straight path.

Italy has four active volcanoes, including Vesuvius, near Naples, and Etna, Europe's highest volcano, on Sicily.

The Tower of Pisa (below) is the bell tower of the Cathedral. Building began in 1173 and it took about 200 years to complete. It was already leaning when the building was finished. Its inclination and its beauty have made it one of Italy's most visited sites. Today it costs the Italian government more to keep the Tower of Pisa leaning than it would to straighten it.

Q&A

Q: Why are Italian restaurants found in most countries?

A: Poverty forced many Italians to emigrate to other countries and they found that their cooking was enjoyed wherever they went.

Q: What is the national sport of Italy?

A: Soccer. Italy won the World Cup in 1934, 1938, 1982 and 2006.

43

Spain

Almudena's cathedral in Madrid (left) has an interesting history. Plans for the building began in the 16th century, but construction did not begin until the 1800s. It was not completed until 1993, when the cathedral was consecrated by Pope John Paul II.

Spain occupies 85% of the land known as the Iberian Peninsula, which it shares with Portugal, in southwest Europe. Africa is fewer than 10 miles (16 km) away to the south across the Strait of Gibraltar and it is bordered by France and Andorra to the north. The Balearic Islands (Majorca, Ibiza and Menorca) lie off Spain's east coast in the Mediterranean Sea. They are very popular tourist resorts, as are the Canary Islands of Tenerife and Gran Canaria which lie 62 miles (100 km) west of Africa.

Paella (right) is the most famous traditional dish of Spain. The basic ingredients are rice and vegetables and, depending on the wealth of a family, can also include meat or seafood. Saffron gives the rice a yellow colour. The largest paella ever was made in 1992. It had a diameter of 65 ft (20 m) and was eaten by 100,000 people.

Fascinating Facts

Spaniards have three names: a Christian name, and two surnames. A person's first surname is the father's first surname; the second is the mother's first surname. So Picasso's full name was Pablo Ruiz Picasso.

Spain is famous for bullfights (above right). Spanish crowds attend some 17,000 bullfights in the country every year, mostly held in July and August.

Madrid is the capital of Spain. It was selected as the capital only in the second half of the 16th century, and is located in the heart of the country. The city has a population of over three million and is a business centre, headquarters for the public administration, government, Spanish parliament, as well as the home of the Spanish royal family. Madrid is also a major tourist city due to its intense cultural and artistic activity, and has a very lively nightlife.

La Coruña
Gijón
Oviedo
Lugo
Santiago de Compostela
Leó
Vigo
Orense
Baltar   La Gudina
Villa
42°
Zamora
Salamanca
Ciudad Rodrigo
Hoyos   Béjar
40°
Ta
Trujillo
Cáceres
39°
Badajoz   Don B
Azuaga
38°
Constantina
Nerva   Guadalqui
Huelva   Sevilla
37°
Osuna
Arcos
Jerez
Cádiz
36°
Algeciras   C

Spain had one of the most powerful empires during the 16th and 17th centuries and took control, along with Portugal, of much of South America. They eventually lost control of the seas to Britain and subsequently fell behind the northern European countries during the industrial revolution. There followed a period of rapid modernisation and it is now one of the most dynamic economies in the EU (European Union).

Spain produced two of the most famous artists of the 20th century, Pablo Picasso and Salvador Dali. The Art Nouveau architect, Antoni Gaudi, left a great mark on Barcelona with his unique twisted and curvaceous buildings (below).

DATA BANK

Longest river
Ebro 565 miles (910 km)

Highest mountains
Mount Mulhacén 11,424 ft (3,482 m) (mainland) and Pico de Teide 12,198 ft (3,718 m) (Tenerife)

Coastline
3,084 miles (4,964 km)

Climate
Droughts are frequent in all but the Pyrenées. The Pyrenées and Sierra Nevada have winter skiing, but most areas have hot summers.

Largest city and population
Madrid 2,905,100

Annual income
US$23,300 or £13,000 approx. per person

The real name of the Spanish language is Castillian, and this language is spoken throughout Spain. Some areas also speak their own language, such as El Euskera, or the Basque language, is spoken in the northern central area of Spain, and Catalan is spoken in Catalonia in northeastern Spain. The people of Andorra, the tiny mountainous country on the northern border of Spain, also speak Catalan.

Q&A

Q: Why is Spain the world's second most popular tourist destination?

A: It is no more than three hours' flight from the densely populated areas of northern Europe, so millions of Britons, Germans and Scandinavians flock to its sandy beaches, attracted by the warm sunny weather, low cost of living and historic towns.

Q: What is flamenco dancing?

A: Flamenco is the traditional song and dance of the gypsies (flamencos) of Andalusia in southern Spain. Flamenco combines acoustic guitar playing, singing, chanting, dancing and staccato handclapping.

Map labels: Bilbao, San Sebastián, Vitoria, Pamplona, Burgos, Logroño, Soria, Saragossa, Ebro, Duero, Figueras, Gerona, Tarrasa, Lérida, Barcelona, Caspe, Tarragona, SPAIN, del Campo, Tortosa, Morella, Vinaroz, Segovia, Tajo, Guadalajara, Teruel, Menorca, Mallorca, Mahón, Madrid, Cuenca, Palma, Manacor, Aranjuez, Saguneto, Requena, Valencia, Júcar, Villarrobledo, Alcira, Ibiza, BALLEARIC ISLANDS, Albacete, Ibiza, Alcoy, Formentera, Alcaraz, Yecla, Real, Alicante, Puertollano, Moratalla, Cieza, Murcia, Jaén, Lorca, Cartagena, Alcala la Real, Huércal Overa, Granada, Mt. Mulhacen 11,424 ft 3,482 m, Almería, Berja, alaga

0 30 60 90 120 miles

0 50 100 150 200 kilometres

45

Portugal

P ortugal consists of the south western part of the Iberian Peninsula, and the Atlantic island groups of the Azores and Madeira.

The Azores are a group of nine islands 930 miles (1,500 km) from Lisbon. The Azores are really the tops of some of the highest mountains in the world, if measured from the bottom of the sea. The islands are of volcanic origin, the most recent eruption being in 1957.

Despite their rich, seafaring past, superb beach resorts, historic towns and landscape wreathed in olive groves, vineyards and wheat fields, Portuguese workers earn only half the European average. Most people still work in agriculture, with food and animal products such as leather goods, cork products, canned fish (anchovies, sardines, and tuna), wine, paper, and olive oil being exported worldwide (below). The warm, sunny climate of the coastal areas plus the low cost of living has made tourism a growing industry.

DATA BANK

Longest river
Tajo 584 miles (940 km)

Highest mountains
Malhão de Estrela 6,532 ft (1,991 m) (mainland) and Ponta do Pico (Azores) 7,713 ft (2,351 m)

Coastline
1,114 miles (1,793 km)

Climate
Northern mountains are wet, with 90 inches (230 cm), but the lowland south is dry, with only 16 inches of rain (40 cm). The south has hot summers and frost-free winters. The northeast can be snowy in winter with hot summers.

Largest city and population
Lisbon 558,100

Annual income
US $17,900 or £10,000 approx. per person

In the last 30 years, long droughts have caused over half of Portugal's farmland to become very dry, causing a drop in farm production (above).

500 years ago Portugal was one of the world's richest countries, and the Portuguese language is still spoken by more than 150 million people throughout Brazil, and former Portuguese colonies in Africa and East Asia.

ATLANTIC OCEAN

Braga

Porto
Tâmega
Lamego

Ovar
Aviero
Vis

Malhão de Es
6,532 ft
1,991 m

Coimbra

Leiria
Tomar
Tagus

Caldas da Rainha

Santarém
Po

P O R T U G

Lisbon
Setúbal
Évo

Beja

Guadiana

Lagos
Faro

0	15	30	45	60 miles
0	25	50	75	100 kilometres

46

7°   6°

Tuela

• Bragança

• Mogadouro

uro

• Pinhel

• Guarda

ã

Portugal's capital Lisbon is situated on the north banks of the River Tagus. The city's historic centre is built on seven hills, making some of the streets too steep for motor vehicles.The city is served by a tram system that is almost 100 years old, complete with original tram cars, one lift, and three funicular services. A funicular is a railway that travels up (and down) a very steep incline. Cables are attached to the adjacent tram-like carriages and as one tram travels up the other travels down. If there is only one tram it is winched by gears.

Madeira is a popular resort (especially famous for its wine), which was occupied by the Portugese in 1418 when they were at the height of their power. The Romans called them the Purple Islands because that is how they appear in the distance.

The Portugese are great seafaring people who discovered large parts of the world, opened up trade routes to India, and were the first to sail round the treacherous Cape of Good Hope in 1487.

As Portugal faces the Atlantic it has a milder climate than Spain. It is divided by the River Tagus. To the north it is mountainous with plateaus which allow agriculture to take place. South of the Tagus it is mostly rolling plains, and in the extreme south separated from the rest by mountains is the Algarve which has a Mediterranean climate comparable to Spain.

Fascinating Facts

Portugal accounts for 33% of the world's cork-oak trees (left). The forest covers an area of 1,791,514 acres (725,000 hectares) and is responsible for 51% of world production of the cork used in wine bottles and floor tiles.

The world's largest single cork tree grows in Portugal (left). On average it yields over 2,205 lb (1,000 kg) of raw cork per harvest, which is enough cork for 100,000 wine bottles, over 25 times the yield from an average cork tree.

Port wine hails from the Portuguese city of Porto.

Belém Tower, or Torre de Belém (above), is a five-storey fortified lighthouse located in Lisbon. It was constructed in the 1500s. The tower stood on an island in the middle of the River Tagus, then in the late 1700s the course of the river was diverted by an earthquake. It is now classified as a World Heritage site.

Q&A

Q: Who was Vasco da Gama?

A: Vasco da Gama was a Portuguese explorer who, in 1498, discovered an ocean route from Portugal to India.

Q: What is the most popular Portuguese seafood?

A: Sardines (left). The average annual consumption is 155 lb (70 kg) per person. That's over 1,200 sardines each year!

Madeira

0   30 miles
0   50 kilometres

Azores

° Corvo
Flores
Graciosa
Terceira
São Jorge
Faial
Pico
São Miguel

0   30 miles
0   50 kilometres

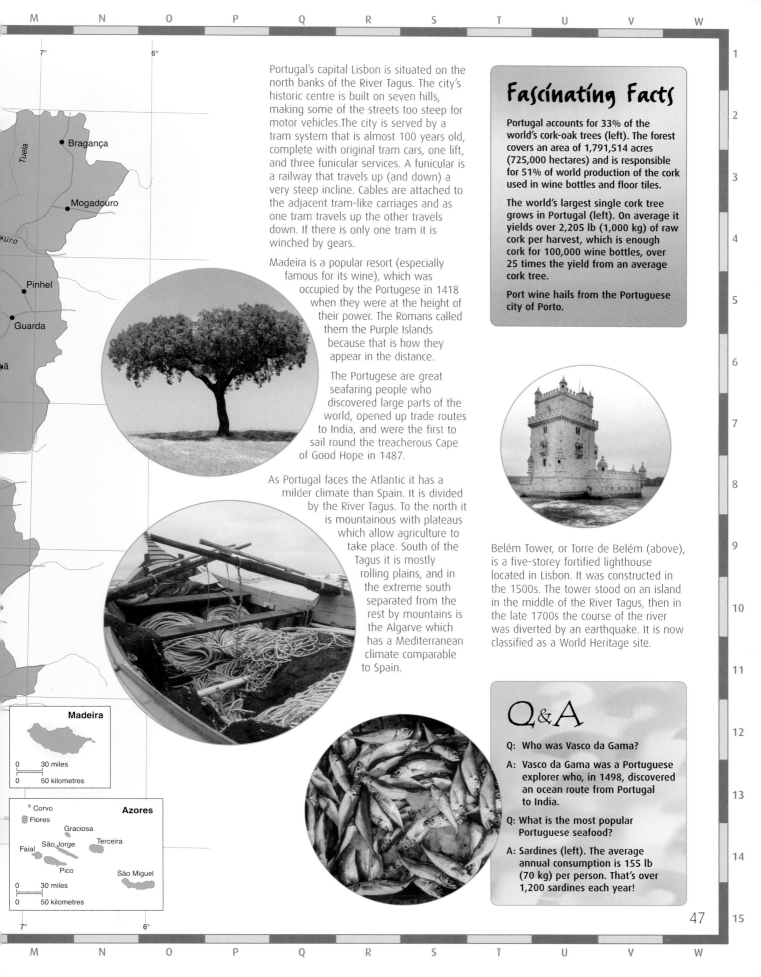

Central Europe

Poland, Slovakia, the Czech Republic and Hungary, which make up this newly democratic region, are amongst the newest members of the European Union. Standards of living are much lower than in Western Europe, and many workers have moved to Ireland, Britain and Germany for better-paid jobs. Poland and Hungary are mainly flat with cool summers. The Carpathian Mountains divide Poland from Slovakia.

Czech Republic

The Czech Republic and Slovakia were created in 1993 by dividing the country of Czechoslovakia, which was Communist until 1989. Prague, the Czech Republic's beautiful capital, situated on the Vltava River, has long been an intellectual and cultural centre and is visited by over 10 million tourists per year. Scientist Albert Einstein taught at Charles-Ferdinand University and the city is home to fine palaces and churches.

Slovakia

Slovakia's capital, Bratislava, lies on both banks of the River Danube at the southwestern edge of the country. Just a few minutes away by car or train are the borders of both Austria and Hungary. Most Slovaks live in small towns and villages where their traditional folk culture is still preserved. The mountainous region in the north of the country is a popular tourist venue during the winter season. It is also idyllic walking country

Poland

Northern Poland is industrialised, with steelworks and shipyards on the Baltic coast and coal mines inland. European Union membership has enabled new industries (such as a Volkswagen car factory) to be built, but in the countryside, horse-drawn carts are still commonly used.

Hungary

Hungary became Communist after World War II, but held democratic elections in 1990. The graceful capital Budapest has a lively arts, cafe and music scene, and is host to a range of cultural and sporting festivals. The countryside is scenic with many lakes, historic towns and rustic villages. Budapest only became a single city in 1873 when Buda on the right bank of the Danube joined with Pest on the left bank.

Fascinating Facts

The largest meteor ever to hit Europe landed near the small town of Zboj in East Slovakia in 1866.

Bratislava is the only capital in the world which borders two countries – Austria and Hungary.

Under the town of Wieliczka in Poland is one of the world's oldest operating salt mines. The mine is so large that it has an underground church, buildings, lakes and passages.

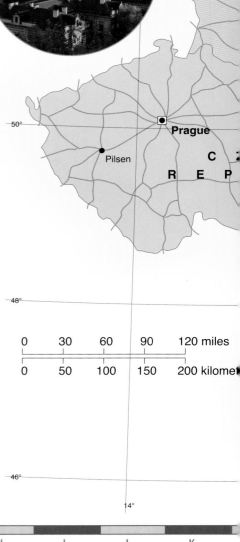

Baltic

N

Szczecin

Ode

50°

Prague

Pilsen

C

R E P

48°

| 0 | 30 | 60 | 90 | 120 miles |

| 0 | 50 | 100 | 150 | 200 kilomet |

46°

14°

14°

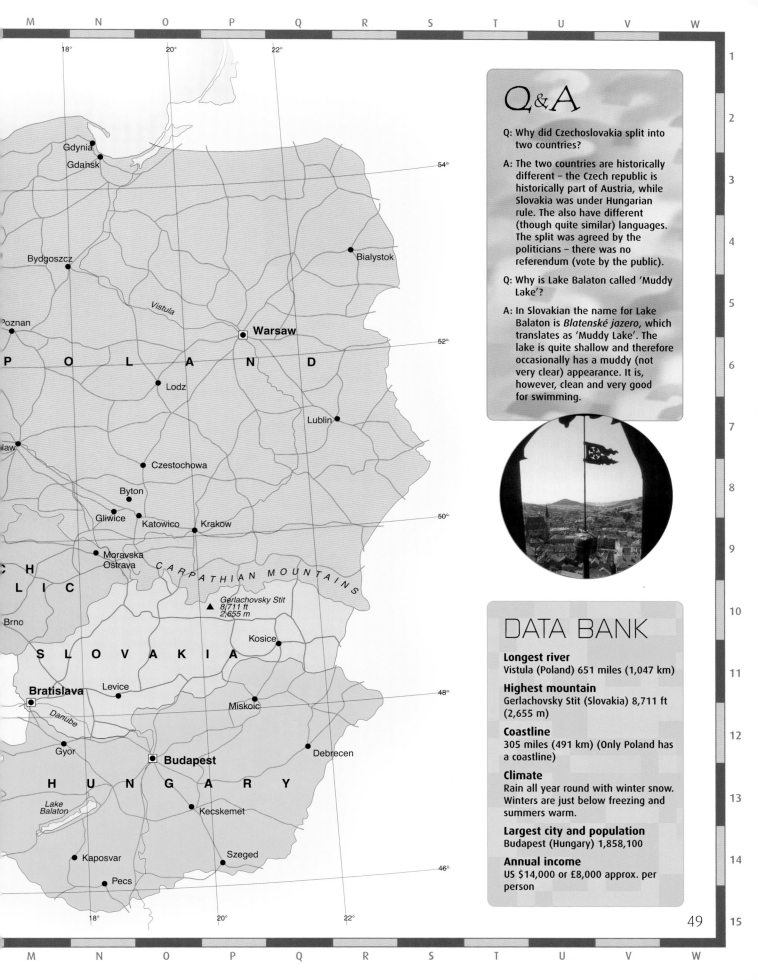

Gdynia
Gdansk

Bydgoszcz

Bialystok

Poznan

P O L A N D

Vistula

□ Warsaw

Lodz

Lublin

aw

Czestochowa

Byton

Gliwice
Katowico   Krakow

Moravska
Ostrava

Brno

C A R P A T H I A N   M O U N T A I N S

▲ Gerlachovsky Stit
8,711 ft
2,655 m

Kosice

S L O V A K I A

Levice

Bratislava
□

Miskoic

Danube

Gyor

□ Budapest

Debrecen

H U N G A R Y

Lake
Balaton

Kecskemet

Kaposvar

Szeged

Pecs

C
H

L
I
C

18°   20°   22°

54°

52°

50°

48°

46°

Q&A

Q: Why did Czechoslovakia split into two countries?

A: The two countries are historically different – the Czech republic is historically part of Austria, while Slovakia was under Hungarian rule. The also have different (though quite similar) languages. The split was agreed by the politicians – there was no referendum (vote by the public).

Q: Why is Lake Balaton called 'Muddy Lake'?

A: In Slovakian the name for Lake Balaton is *Blatenské jazero*, which translates as 'Muddy Lake'. The lake is quite shallow and therefore occasionally has a muddy (not very clear) appearance. It is, however, clean and very good for swimming.

DATA BANK

Longest river
Vistula (Poland) 651 miles (1,047 km)

Highest mountain
Gerlachovsky Stit (Slovakia) 8,711 ft (2,655 m)

Coastline
305 miles (491 km) (Only Poland has a coastline)

Climate
Rain all year round with winter snow. Winters are just below freezing and summers warm.

Largest city and population
Budapest (Hungary) 1,858,100

Annual income
US $14,000 or £8,000 approx. per person

South-eastern Europe

Of the nations of Slovenia, Croatia, Bosnia and Herzegovina, Serbia, Montenegro, Macedonia and Albania, all but Albania were part of Yugoslavia until 1999. Geographically and culturally they are a very varied group of countries. From the alpine north of Slovenia to the marvellous Mediterranean climate of the Croatian coast. Inland there are rugged and barren mountains. Beyond the mountains there are extensive arable plains near the Danube, where vegetables and grain are harvested.

Since its separation from Montenegro in June 2006, the country of Serbia finds itself landlocked. It shares many borders; with Albania, Montenegro, Bosnia and Herzegovina, Bulgaria, Croatia, Hungary, the Republic of Macedonia, and Romania. The Danube River provides shipping access to inland Europe and the Black Sea.

Macedonia is a country full of medieval monasteries, vineyards, orchards, bazaars and Turkish-style food. It is called the country of lakes and mountains. The capital city is Skopje, situated near the northern border with Serbia.

The hot summers of the Croatian and Slovenian coastal region are very well suited to growing grapes and there is a thriving wine industry (below right).

Zagreb is the capital of Croatia. The city was unspoilt by the recent wars, and is a bustling commercial centre.

DATA BANK

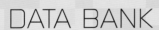

Longest river
Sava (Slovenia, Croatia, Bosnia and Herzegovina, Serbia and Montenegro) 587 miles (945 km)

Highest mountain
Korab (on the border of Macedonia and Albania) 9,068 ft (2764 m)

Coastline
3,667 miles (5,901 km)

Climate
Dry summers and wet winters. Very wet in the mountains. Hot summers on the coast and in the south. Cold, snowy winters in the interior mountains.

Largest city and population
Belgrade (Serbia) 1,280,600

Annual income
US $5,000 or £2,500 approx. per person

The Plitvice Lakes of Croatia (below right) – a series of 16 beautiful lakes and tarns of crystal blue-green colour, one below another – are a World Heritage site. Between the lakes there are many marvellous waterfalls and cascades. The exceptional beauty of the lakes and waterfalls, the rich plant and animal life, contrasting colours, forests and pure mountain air attract nature lovers from all over the world.

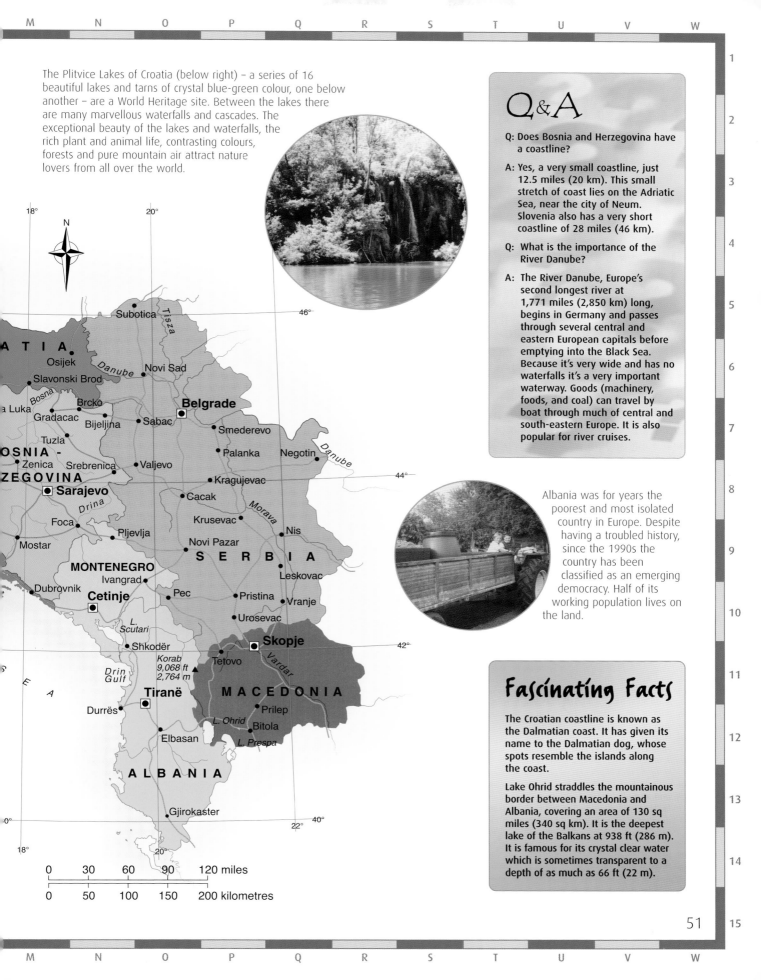

Q & A

Q: Does Bosnia and Herzegovina have a coastline?

A: Yes, a very small coastline, just 12.5 miles (20 km). This small stretch of coast lies on the Adriatic Sea, near the city of Neum. Slovenia also has a very short coastline of 28 miles (46 km).

Q: What is the importance of the River Danube?

A: The River Danube, Europe's second longest river at 1,771 miles (2,850 km) long, begins in Germany and passes through several central and eastern European capitals before emptying into the Black Sea. Because it's very wide and has no waterfalls it's a very important waterway. Goods (machinery, foods, and coal) can travel by boat through much of central and south-eastern Europe. It is also popular for river cruises.

Albania was for years the poorest and most isolated country in Europe. Despite having a troubled history, since the 1990s the country has been classified as an emerging democracy. Half of its working population lives on the land.

Fascinating Facts

The Croatian coastline is known as the Dalmatian coast. It has given its name to the Dalmatian dog, whose spots resemble the islands along the coast.

Lake Ohrid straddles the mountainous border between Macedonia and Albania, covering an area of 130 sq miles (340 sq km). It is the deepest lake of the Balkans at 938 ft (286 m). It is famous for its crystal clear water which is sometimes transparent to a depth of as much as 66 ft (22 m).

Map labels:

18° 20° 22° 40° 42° 44° 46°

N

Subotica
Tisza
ATIA
Osijek
Danube
Novi Sad
Slavonski Brod
Bosna
a Luka
Brcko
Gradacac
Bijeljina
Sabac
Belgrade
Smederevo
Tuzla
Palanka
Negotin
Danube
OSNIA -
Zenica
Srebrenica
Valjevo
Kragujevac
ZEGOVINA
Sarajevo
Cacak
Drina
Krusevac
Morava
Foca
Nis
Mostar
Pljevlja
Novi Pazar
S E R B I A
MONTENEGRO
Leskovac
Ivangrad
Dubrovnik
Pec
Pristina
Vranje
Cetinje
Urosevac
L. Scutari
Shkodër
Skopje
Korab 9,068 ft 2,764 m
Tetovo
Vardar
Drin Gulf
M A C E D O N I A
Tiranë
Durrës
Prilep
L. Ohrid
Bitola
Elbasan
L. Prespa
A L B A N I A
Gjirokaster

0 30 60 90 120 miles
0 50 100 150 200 kilometres

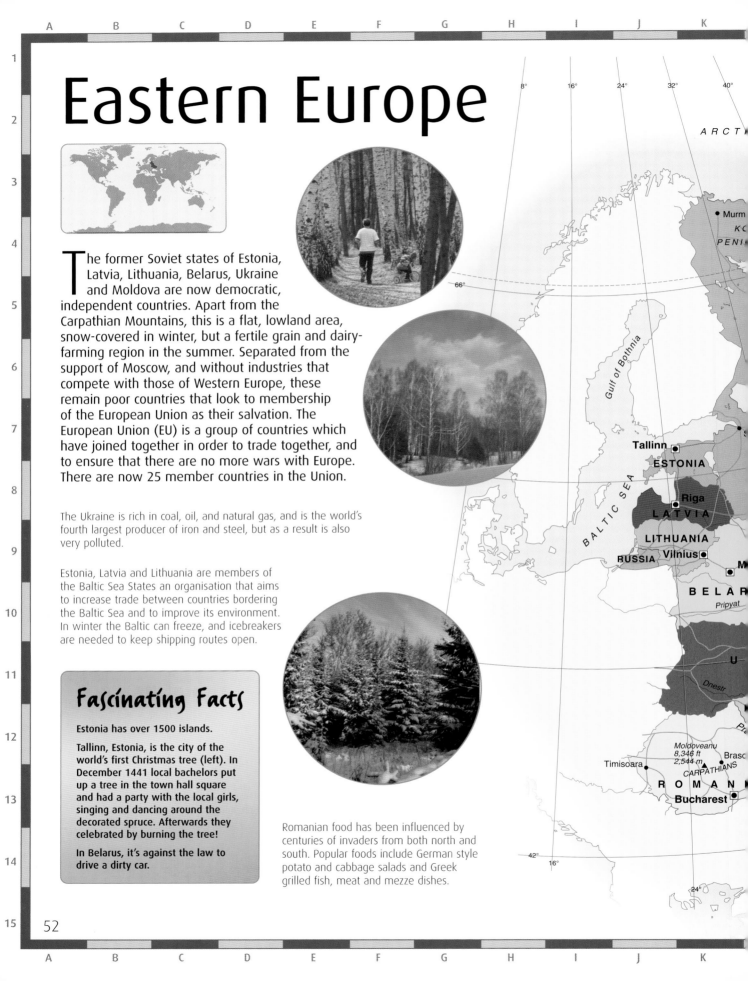

Eastern Europe

The former Soviet states of Estonia, Latvia, Lithuania, Belarus, Ukraine and Moldova are now democratic, independent countries. Apart from the Carpathian Mountains, this is a flat, lowland area, snow-covered in winter, but a fertile grain and dairy-farming region in the summer. Separated from the support of Moscow, and without industries that compete with those of Western Europe, these remain poor countries that look to membership of the European Union as their salvation. The European Union (EU) is a group of countries which have joined together in order to trade together, and to ensure that there are no more wars with Europe. There are now 25 member countries in the Union.

The Ukraine is rich in coal, oil, and natural gas, and is the world's fourth largest producer of iron and steel, but as a result is also very polluted.

Estonia, Latvia and Lithuania are members of the Baltic Sea States an organisation that aims to increase trade between countries bordering the Baltic Sea and to improve its environment. In winter the Baltic can freeze, and icebreakers are needed to keep shipping routes open.

Fascinating Facts

Estonia has over 1500 islands.

Tallinn, Estonia, is the city of the world's first Christmas tree (left). In December 1441 local bachelors put up a tree in the town hall square and had a party with the local girls, singing and dancing around the decorated spruce. Afterwards they celebrated by burning the tree!

In Belarus, it's against the law to drive a dirty car.

Romanian food has been influenced by centuries of invaders from both north and south. Popular foods include German style potato and cabbage salads and Greek grilled fish, meat and mezze dishes.

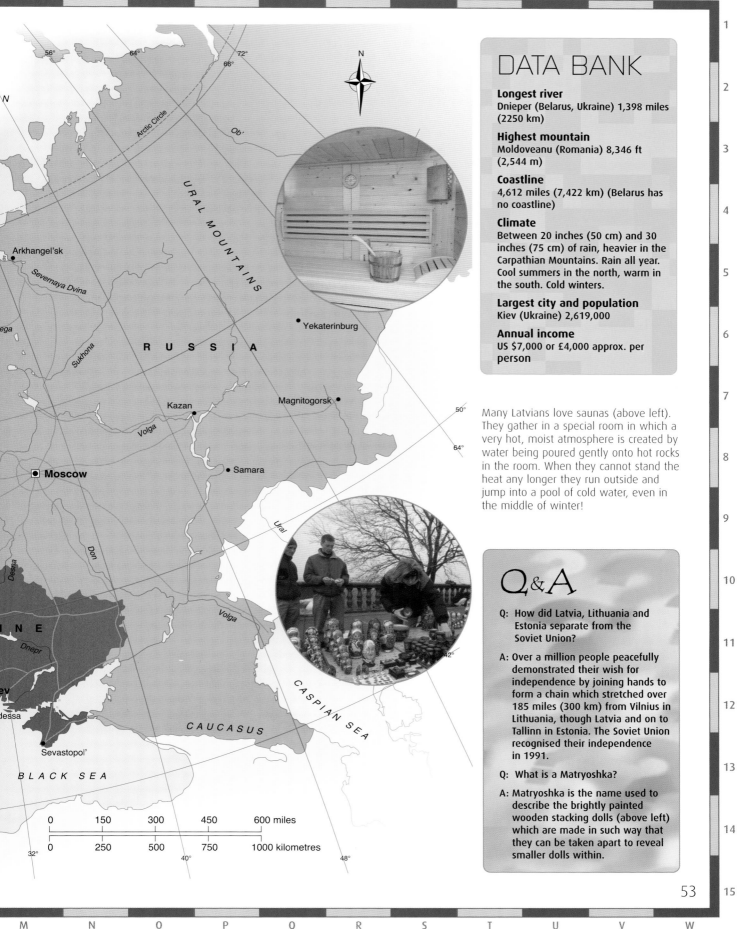

56° 64° 72° 66°

N

Ob'

Arctic Circle

URAL MOUNTAINS

Arkhangel'sk

Severnaya Dvina

Onega

Sukhona

R U S S I A

Yekaterinburg

Kazan

Volga

Magnitogorsk

50°

64°

Moscow

Samara

Ural

Desna

Don

Volga

N E

Dnepr

 nev

Odessa

C A U C A S U S

CASPIAN SEA

42°

Sevastopol'

B L A C K   S E A

0	150	300	450	600 miles
0	250	500	750	1000 kilometres

32° 40° 48°

DATA BANK

Longest river
Dnieper (Belarus, Ukraine) 1,398 miles (2250 km)

Highest mountain
Moldoveanu (Romania) 8,346 ft (2,544 m)

Coastline
4,612 miles (7,422 km) (Belarus has no coastline)

Climate
Between 20 inches (50 cm) and 30 inches (75 cm) of rain, heavier in the Carpathian Mountains. Rain all year. Cool summers in the north, warm in the south. Cold winters.

Largest city and population
Kiev (Ukraine) 2,619,000

Annual income
US $7,000 or £4,000 approx. per person

Many Latvians love saunas (above left). They gather in a special room in which a very hot, moist atmosphere is created by water being poured gently onto hot rocks in the room. When they cannot stand the heat any longer they run outside and jump into a pool of cold water, even in the middle of winter!

Q&A

Q: How did Latvia, Lithuania and Estonia separate from the Soviet Union?

A: Over a million people peacefully demonstrated their wish for independence by joining hands to form a chain which stretched over 185 miles (300 km) from Vilnius in Lithuania, though Latvia and on to Tallinn in Estonia. The Soviet Union recognised their independence in 1991.

Q: What is a Matryoshka?

A: Matryoshka is the name used to describe the brightly painted wooden stacking dolls (above left) which are made in such way that they can be taken apart to reveal smaller dolls within.

Greece

Greece has a history stretching back almost 4,000 years. The people of the mainland, called Hellenes, explored the Mediterranean and the Black Sea, going as far as the Atlantic Ocean and the Caucasus Mountains. Numerous Greek settlements were founded throughout the Mediterranean, Asia and the coast of North Africa as a result of travels in search of new markets.

Greece was the greatest European civilisation from 1000 BC to 300 BC and this has left a heritage that includes the Parthenon in Athens, and Olympia, site of the first Olympic games in 776 BC. The Olympic Games was the greatest national festival for the Athenians. Held every four years, athletes came from all regions of Greece to compete in the great Stadium of Olympia.

DATA BANK

Longest river
Aliákmon 185 miles (297 km)

Highest mountain
Mount Olympos 9,570 ft (2,917 m)

Coastline
8,498 miles (13,676 km)

Climate
From more than 47 inches (120 cm) in the mountains to less than 16 inches (40 cm) on the coast. Summers are hot and winters mild, with mountain snow.

Largest city and population
Athens 757,400

Annual income
US $21,300 or £12,000 approx. per person

Fascinating Facts

The Corinth Canal (right) connects the Gulf of Corinth with the Aegean Sea, thus saving a 248 miles (400 km) long journey. Unfortunately, since it is only 69 ft (21 m) wide, it is too narrow for modern ocean freighters!

In Greece almost every house has solar cell panels on the roof. These panels convert sunlight into electricity.

The Marathon race is named after a battle in 489 BC when the Greeks beat the Persian army. To get word back to Athens as soon as possible, a young soldier ran the entire distance, 26 miles (42 km), shouted 'We have won!' and fell dead of exhaustion.

More than 80% of Greece is mountainous. Winters are mild and summers hot and dry. Agriculture is the most important economic activity, with cultivation being mainly by farmers using traditional methods. The dry climate, steep slopes and thin soil limit what can be grown to grapes, olives, citrus fruit, and to the keeping of sheep and goats. However agriculture still involves around 20% of the population and the country exports agricultural products, which account for a significant part of Greek income.

Edhessa
Florina
Ná
Kastoría
Kozáni
Neápolis
Aliákm
Mou
9,57
2,91
Elassón
Kérkira
Ioánnina
Trikkala
Piniós
Kérkira
Akhelóös
Kardhítsa
Párga
Arta
G R E E C
Préveza
Levkás
Pálairos
Agrínion
Levkás
Astakós
Thérmon
Kefallinía
Ithláki
Mesalóngion
Sámi
Pátrai
Aíyion
Gu
Zákinthos
Amaliás
Lambia
Zákinthos
Pírgos
Olympia
Alfios
Trípolis
Megalópolis
Filiatrá
Kalamáta
Pílos
Areópolis
Pírgos

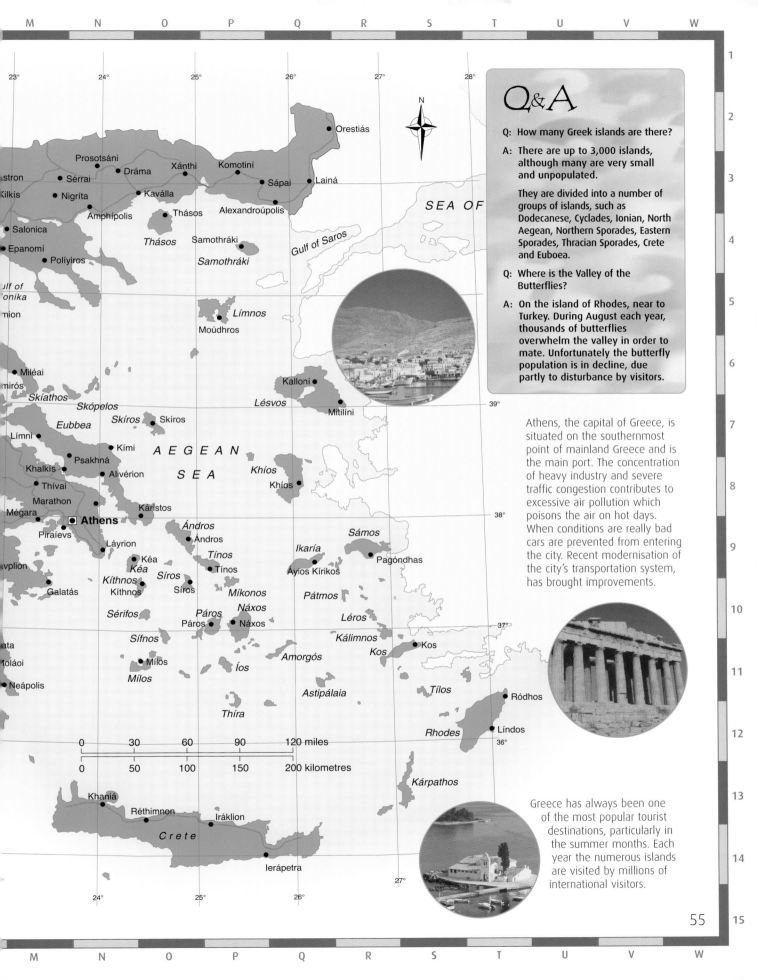

23° 24° 25° 26° 27° 28°

Orestiás

Prosotsáni
Dráma
Xánthi
Komotiní
stron
Sérrai
Sápai
Lainá
Kilkís
Nigríta
Kaválla
Salonica
Amphípolis
Thásos
Alexandroúpolis
Epanomí
Thásos
Samothráki
Políyiros
Samothráki
ulf of
onika
Gulf of Saros
mion

SEA OF

Límnos
Moúdhros

Miléai
mirós
Skíathos
Skópelos
Kalloní
Lésvos
Eubbea
Skíros
Skíros
Mitilíni
Límni
Kími
Psakhná
A E G E A N
Khíos
Khalkís
Alivérion
Khíos
Thívai
S E A
Marathon
Kárlstos
Mégara
Athens
Piraíevs
Sámos
Láyrion
Ándros
Ikaría
vplion
Ándros
Ayios Kírikos
Pagóndhas
Kéa
Tínos
Galatás
Kéa
Síros
Kíthnos
Tínos
Pátmos
Kíthnos
Síros
Míkonos
Léros
Sérifos
Náxos
Páros
Náxos
Kálimnos
Kos
Sífnos
Kos
Kos
ata
Milos
Amorgós
Moláoi
Mílos
Íos
Tílos
Neápolis
Astipálaia
Ródhos
Thíra
Rhodes
Líndos

39°
38°
37°
36°

Kárpathos

Khaniá
Réthimnon
Iráklion
C r e t e
Ierápetra

0   30   60   90   120 miles
0   50   100   150   200 kilometres

24° 25° 26° 27°

Athens, the capital of Greece, is situated on the southernmost point of mainland Greece and is the main port. The concentration of heavy industry and severe traffic congestion contributes to excessive air pollution which poisons the air on hot days. When conditions are really bad cars are prevented from entering the city. Recent modernisation of the city's transportation system, has brought improvements.

Greece has always been one of the most popular tourist destinations, particularly in the summer months. Each year the numerous islands are visited by millions of international visitors.

Bulgaria

Bulgaria borders the Black Sea. A large proportion of the country, 38%, consists of forests and woodlands. Another 40% is farmland and the rest is mountainous, apart from the land by the River Danube. The country is mainly rural and relatively undeveloped; 20% of the country's small population live in Sofia, the capital.

Roughly 25% of Bulgarians are farmers, usually working very small plots to produce food for themselves and for local markets. Roses are one of the few commercial crops; their petals are used in the perfume industry. Around 30% of people work in industry – making coke, refined petroleum, chemicals, fertilisers, metals, and machinery such as forklift trucks. Government, education, health and the retail sector are large employers, and tourism is becoming increasingly important as the Black Sea resort (right) and skiing holidays in the mountains increase in popularity. Western Europeans have been buying holiday homes, in what is, for them, a low-cost country.

DATA BANK

Longest river
Iskur 229 miles (368 km)

Highest mountain
Musala 9,595 ft (2,925 m)

Coastline
220 miles (354 km)

Climate
Temperate. Cold, damp winters. Hot, dry summers.

Largest city and population
Sofia 1,194,164

Annual income
US $9,600 or £5,000 approx. per person

Bulgaria's food is similar to that of Greece and Turkey, and includes stuffed vegetables, kebabs, spicy sausages and cheese dishes, which are usually served with rice and bulgar wheat. Yoghurt is also popular – Bulgaria is said to be the home of yoghurt. Desserts tend to be sweetened with honey, and include pancakes, baked apples, fruit and baklava (right). Baklava is a rich, sweet pastry made with nuts.

26°   27°   28°

44°

● Ruse

● Svishtov   ● Razgrad   Dobrich ●

● Shumen   Balchik

Turgovishte   Varna ●

Kamchiya

43°

L   G   A   R   I   A

● Kazanluk   Sliven ●

Tundzha

● StaraZagora   ● Yambol   ● Burgas

● Chirpan

Maritsa ● Dimitrovgrad

● Khaskovo

yan

26°   27°   28°

41°

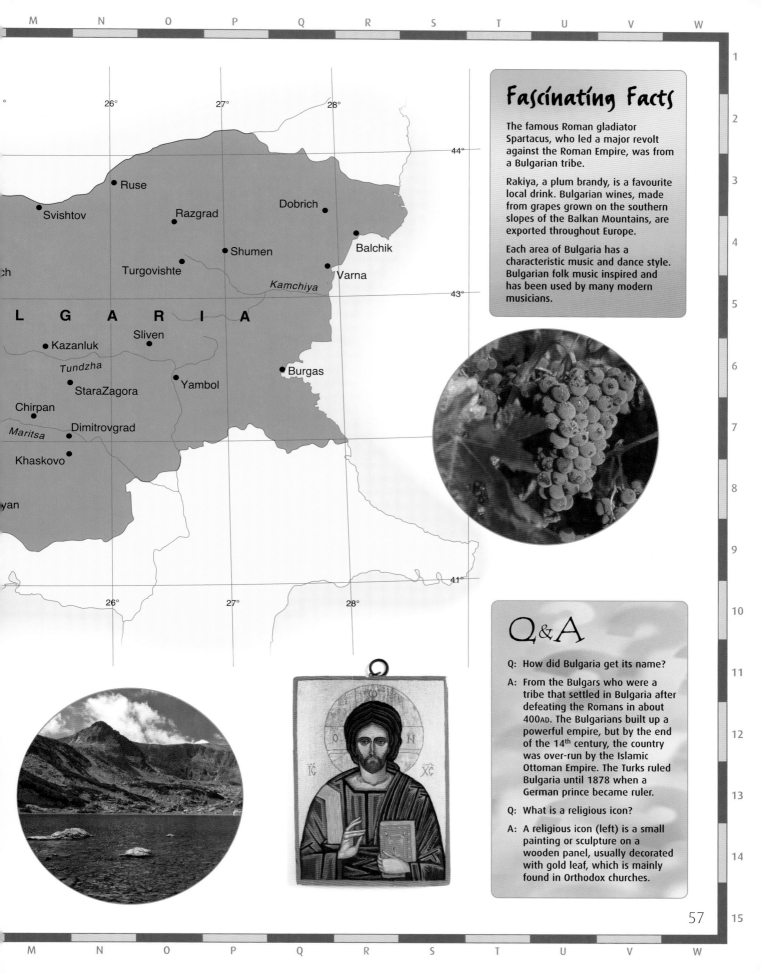

Fascinating Facts

The famous Roman gladiator Spartacus, who led a major revolt against the Roman Empire, was from a Bulgarian tribe.

Rakiya, a plum brandy, is a favourite local drink. Bulgarian wines, made from grapes grown on the southern slopes of the Balkan Mountains, are exported throughout Europe.

Each area of Bulgaria has a characteristic music and dance style. Bulgarian folk music inspired and has been used by many modern musicians.

Q&A

Q: How did Bulgaria get its name?

A: From the Bulgars who were a tribe that settled in Bulgaria after defeating the Romans in about 400AD. The Bulgarians built up a powerful empire, but by the end of the 14th century, the country was over-run by the Islamic Ottoman Empire. The Turks ruled Bulgaria until 1878 when a German prince became ruler.

Q: What is a religious icon?

A: A religious icon (left) is a small painting or sculpture on a wooden panel, usually decorated with gold leaf, which is mainly found in Orthodox churches.

Russia west of the Urals

E uropean Russia, to the west of the Ural Mountains, contains the major cities and industries of the former Communist Soviet Union. Since 1991, when Communism collapsed, the western regions of Ukraine, Belarus, Estonia and Latvia have become independent nations and Russia has struggled to improve the standard of living for the majority of its citizens.

The country has cold winters, but is a fertile agricultural region and is rich in natural resources. This former superpower controls much of Europe's natural gas supplies, but is troubled by internal terrorism from some regions, such as the southern Chechen region, where the people are seeking independence.

Dance is an important part of Russian culture. There are many famous Russian dance groups, including the Bolshoi ballet, the Cossacks and the Georgian folk dancers (below).

Russia is famous for caviar – the eggs from the sturgeon. In Russia, caviar is eaten on blinis (thin buckwheat pancakes), or on toast, often accompanied by vodka. The international demand is so great that it is now a luxury item, and due to dam building, poaching and pollution, the sturgeon could become extinct.

Giving Easter eggs is a Russian tradition. Some are made of chocolate, some are real eggs, but the most famous are those designed by Carl Fabergé for the Russian royal family 100 years ago. These were made out of fine porcelain and painted and decorated with gold and jewels (left).

Q&A

Q: Where does the name Red Square come from?

A: The name of Red Square in Russian is Krasnaya ploshchad. Originally Krasnaya translated as 'red' or 'beautiful' and so Krasnaya ploshchad meant Beautiful Square. Over many years the Russian word krasnaya ceased to be used for beautiful and so Krasnaya ploshchad now means Red Square.

Q: What is the Kremlin?

A: Russia's parliament and government buildings are housed in the Kremlin in Moscow, which dates from 1331.

Domes (below) are an impressive feature of Russian architecture. Examples include the Archangel Cathedral, the Cathedral of the Annunciation and Moscow's Kremlin

Fascinating Facts

The largest lake in the world is the Caspian Sea which is 760 miles (1,225 km) long. Its area is 143,550 sq miles (371,800 sq km).

St. Petersburg is sometimes called the 'Venice of the North' as it has many canals and hundreds of bridges.

In 1917 the Russian Revolution overthrew the royal family and Vladimir Ilyich Lenin led the Communist revolution that established the USSR. When he died in 1924 his body was embalmed and put on public display in Moscow – where it remains to this day!

0 250 300 450 600 miles
0 200 400 600 800 1000 kilometres

N

BARENTS SEA

Murmansk

Arkhangel'sk

Severnaya Dvina

Ob'

Ob'

Irtysh

Irtysh

R U S S I A

U
R
A
L
S

Sukhona

Omsk

St Petersburg

Yekaterinburg

Tobol

ESTONIA

LATVIA

LITHUANIA

RUSSIA

Kazan

Volga

Magnitogorsk

Moscow

BELARUS

Samara

Desna

Don

K A Z A K H S T A N

Ural

U K R A I N E

Volga

UZBEKISTAN

CASPIAN SEA

Mt Elbrus
18,510
5,642 m

BLACK SEA

GEORGIA

AZERBAIJAN

ARMENIA

North America

S tretching from the ice of the Arctic Ocean to Mexico, North America is a continent of contrasts.

The native people of North America originally came across the frozen Arctic Ocean from Asia, but centuries of immigration from Europe, Africa and southeast Asia have made the USA and Canada a multi-cultural society.

DATA BANK

Longest river
Mackenzie (Canada) 2,635 miles
(4,241 km)

Highest mountain
Mount McKinley (United States)
20,322 ft (6,194 m)

Climate
The climate ranges from the icy cold Arctic in the north of Canada to the hot and dry desert in the midwestern United States, to the humid Caribbean climate in the south.

Natural Resources
Oil, gas, coal, gold

Population
328,539,721

Richest / poorest country
United States of America is the richest country, although Canada is not far behind.

ARCTIC OCEAN

ALASKA

Mt McKinley 29,322 ft ▲ (6,194 m)● Anchorage

C A

Alaska was part of Russia until 1867, when it was bought by the USA for US $7.2 million (or £3,900,000 approx.). The America people thought it a waste of money, not knowing of the vast oil and gold reserves at the time!

● Vancouver

● Seattle

NORTH PACIFIC OCEAN

San Francisco ●

U N I T E

O F

Los Angeles ●

The Old Faithful Geyser in Yellowstone National Park U.S.A. is perhaps the world's most famous geyser. An eruption can shoot up to 68 pints (32,000 l) of boiling water to a height of up to 180 ft (55 m).

The Great Lakes, on the USA–Canadian border, are the largest group of freshwater lakes on the earth. They contain 20% of the world's fresh water, enough to cover the entire USA to a depth of 10ft (3m).

GREENLAND
(Kalaallit Nunaat)

Arctic Circle

■ Nuuk (Godhaab)

A D A

St John's ●

● g

Ottawa ☐

Chicago ●

● New York

☐ Washington

S T A T E S

R I C A

NORTH
ATLANTIC
OCEAN

● Miami

● allas

| 0 | 300 | 600 | 900 | 1200 miles |
| 0 | 500 | 1000 | 1500 | 2000 kilometres |

The Rocky Mountains are part of a mountain chain that stretches from Alaska to Antarctica and contains ice caps, glaciers and volcanoes.

Fascinating Facts

Canada's eastern-most city, St. John's, Newfoundland, is closer to Prague, capital of the Czech Republic than to Vancouver, Canada.

The world's biggest living tree is the giant sequoia called General Sherman in the Sequoia National Park, California, standing 276 ft (84 m) tall, 36 ft (11 m) in diameter and with a girth of 102 ft (31 m).

In Canada the Inuit (formerly known as Eskimos) govern themselves in the Nunavut province. They have adapted to the harsh environment and often combine modern technology with their traditional lifestyle.

Q&A

Q: Which is the oldest city in North America?

A: St John's. It is the capital of Newfoundland. The first permanent settlers were the British who landed here in the middle of the 18th century. The city's architecture is a wonderful blend of colourful wooden houses, stone and brick churches, colonial buildings and modern commercial structures.

Q: Are the Great Lakes in the United States or Canada?

A: The five Great Lakes are on or near the United States–Canadian border. Lake Michigan (the only one entirely in the United States; it is the second largest in volume. The other four lakes are Lake Superior (the largest and deepest), Lake Huron (the second largest in area), Lake Erie (the smallest in volume and shallowest), and Lake Ontario (the smallest in area). These four lakes form the border between the United States and Canada (the border runs roughly through the middle of the lakes).

Q: Where is the coldest place in North America?

A: Greenland and Yukon, Canada, are among the world's coldest places, with temperatures reaching –80°F (–62°C).

About North America

The countries of North America, capital cities and population:

Canada	Ottawa	31,630,000
USA	Washington DC	295,734,000

Greenland is the world's largest island. Although it is geographically part of the Arctic and therefore associated with North America, it is actually part of Europe. Greenland's settlements are confined to its coastal region. Ice sheet covers 80% of the island. In the 10th century Vikings landed on Greenland having sailed from Iceland. By the 18th century it had come under Danish rule and became fully integrated into Denmark in 1953. As part of Denmark, Greenland joined the European Union (then the European Community) but in 1985 it withdrew over fishing quotas. In 1979 it became self-governing and in 1997 Inuit place names superseded Danish ones.

Alaska is a US state, and by far the largest state in the area. It became the 49th state in 1959.

Famous People

- Sitting Bull (*c.* 1834–90) was born in the Dakota Territory, and was the leader of the Native American Hunkpapa Sioux Indian tribe. During the 19th century settlers from the eastern USA spread out across the continent and began to take over the land of the Native Americans. Many Native American tribes fought against this and Sitting Bull led the Sioux at the famous battle of Little Bighorn in 1876, where he defeated the US Army under Col. George Custer.

- Martin Luther King (1929–68) was a Baptist minister and leader of the Civil Rights movement that campaigned for equal rights for America's black citizens. Born in Atlanta, Georgia, King organised peaceful rallies and marches throughout the USA, most famously the march on Washington in 1963 where he gave his most memorable speech, beginning, 'I have a dream'. Awarded a Nobel Peace Prize in 1964, King was assassinated in 1968.

- Elvis Presley (1935–77) Born in Tupelo, Mississippi, USA. He became one of the world's greatest rock stars. His home, Graceland?(below), has become a place of pilgrimage for his many fans.

Languages

- English is the most widely spoken language, though Spanish is very strong in certain parts of the United States.

- French is an official language of Canada and is widely used in Quebec.

Natural features

- Niagara Falls is a group of massive waterfalls on the border of Canada and the USA, between Lake Ontario and Lake Erie. They are not particularly high, but they are exceptionally wide and very spectacular. They attract about 12 million visitors a year

- The Grand Canyon is the largest canyon in the world. It was created over millions of years by the Colorado River. The canyon is around 277 miles (446 km) long, and about 15 miles (24 km) wide at its widest point.

- Monument Valley is an area of free-standing sandstone rock formations that rise majestically from the desert floor. Up to 1,000 ft (305 m) tall, they create a truly magical desert landscape. The beauty of the area is well documented in films and television commercials. The valley is located along the Utah/Arizona border towards the southeast corner of Utah.

- The Florida Keys have become a popular destination for tourists looking for a tropical vacation. The county is famous for alligators and these too are a great attraction.

Environment

- America is the greatest consumer of power and material goods and has one of the highest standards of living in the world. This in turn produces very high levels of greenhouse gas emissions which the countries are trying to find ways to rectify.

- When Europeans first settled North America the native population was drastically reduced because a number of new diseases were introduced, such as bubonic plague, cholera, typhoid fever and whooping cough.

- Reservations were established in the late 1860s in response to conflicts between settlers and Native American tribes. Relations between settlers and the American Indians had grown worse as the settlers encroached on tribal hunting grounds and natural resources.

- Kilauea on Hawaii, USA, is the world's most active volcano. It has been erupting continuously since 1983 and discharges lava at a rate of 176 cu ft (5 cu m) per second.

- The border between Canada and the USA is the longest undefended border in the world.

- Canada and the USA are of similar size, but much of Canada's vast northern tracts are almost uninhabited, being too cold for agriculture. Most of Canada's population live on the eastern seaboard and along the border with the USA.

Land use

- The Great Plains of North America are flatlands that cover a vast area east of the Rockies in both Canada and the USA. In the USA they include the states of New Mexico, Texas, Oklahoma, Colorado, Kansas. Nebraska, Wyoming, Montana, and North and South Dakota.

- The huge oil fields in Alaska and Texas dominate the land.

- In Canada the plains cover Alberta, Manitoba and Saskatchewan. The Canadian plains are commonly known as the Prairies and are home to great wheat farms.

- Wheat is the most important single crop and the Prairie provinces form one of the greatest growing areas of the world, each year producing more than 90% of Canadian wheat

- The plains were home to herds of bison until they were almost made extinct by hunting.

- Manufacturing industry is concentrated around Chicago and Detroit and the Eastern States.

- The Florida Keys are a string of over 1500 islands in the southeast of the United States, about 15 miles south of Miami. The major industries here are tourism and fishing. Ecotourism is also promoted, with many visitors scuba diving, or travelling on the ferries. The waters surrounding the Keys are part of a protected area known as the Florida Keys National Marine Sanctuary.

Industry

- Canada and the USA are more or less self-sufficient and are world leaders in manufacturing industries. The automobile industry is centred around Detroit, and electronic industries are in Silicon Valley, California. New York is the financial heart of the USA

- Tourism is a great source of income for the USA and Canada. The Great Lakes, Florida, California, the Liberty Bell in Philadelphia, Disneyland, the Grand Canyon and, of course, New York, are the most popular places.

- Many tourists to Canada, and indeed Canadians themselves, take trips to see the Aurora Borealis (below). This is a glow in the northern sky, and is often known as the Northern Lights. It can be very spectacular. Whitehorse, Yukon is considered one of the best places in the world for viewing this natural wonder and the area boasts a high success rate for seeing the lights.

Natural Resources

- Canada and the USA are very rich in a wide range of mineral deposits including oil, gas, coal and gold.

Canada

Canada is the world's second largest country, but vast tracts of the north are almost uninhabited, being too cold for agriculture. The largest cities are Toronto and Montreal in the east, and Vancouver in the west. Canada's diverse tourist attractions include Niagara Falls on the border with the United States, and the stunningly beautiful scenery of the Rocky Mountains. Summers in Canada are generally mild, and winters are long and cold. Canada is one of the world's top 10 richest nations. This industrial economy exports 75% of its goods to the USA and is one of the world's leading wheat producers.

Ottawa, the capital of Canada, is situated on the banks of the River Ottawa in the south east of the country. The city is one of the coldest national capitals in the world with average temperatures below freezing for five months of the year. Over 60 festivals and events take place annually in the city. Every February Ottawa hosts the Winterlude, North America's largest winter festival, site of the longest ice rink in the world – the frozen Rideau Canal – filled with ice skaters (below).

ARCTIC OCEAN

BEAUFORT SEA

Banks Island

Victoria Island

Arctic Circle

Dawson

Yukon Territory

Mt. Logan 19,551 5959m

Whitehorse

MACKENZIE MOUNTAINS

Mackenzie

Norman Wells

Fort Norman

Northern Ter

Yellowknife

Fort Resc

British Columbia

Hazelton

ROCKY MOUNTAINS

Fort Smith

C   A

Prince Rupert

Peace River

Peace

Alberta

Saskatche

QUEEN CHARLOTTE ISLANDS

Edmonton

Prince Albert

Vancouver Island

Calgary

Saskatoon

PACIFIC OCEAN

Vancouver

Victoria

Medicine Hat

Regina

0	300	600	900	1200 miles
0	500	1000	1500	2000 kilometres

Fascinating Facts

Canada was French from 1534 to 1763 and French is still an official language, used widely in Quebec.

The baseball glove was invented in Canada in 1883.

Inuits, the native people of Arctic Canada, have 32 words for snow that can describe its wetness, brightness, or colour.

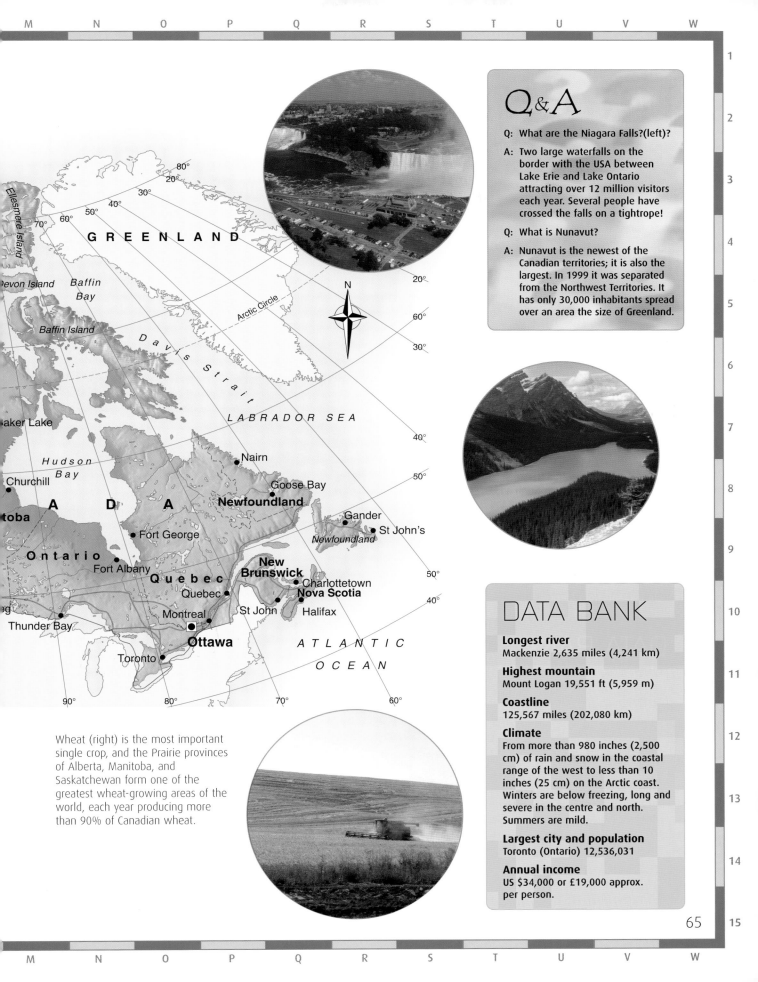

80°
20°
30°
40°
50°
60°
70°

GREENLAND

Ellesmere Island

Devon Island

Baffin Bay

Baffin Island

aker Lake

Hudson Bay

Churchill

A D A

toba

Ontario

Fort Albany

og

Thunder Bay

Toronto

Montreal

Ottawa

Davis Strait

Arctic Circle

20°

N

60°

30°

40°

50°

LABRADOR SEA

Nairn

Goose Bay

Newfoundland

Gander

St John's

Newfoundland

New Brunswick

Charlottetown

Quebec

Nova Scotia

St John

Halifax

Quebec

Fort George

50°

40°

ATLANTIC

OCEAN

90° 80° 70° 60°

Q&A

Q: What are the Niagara Falls?(left)?

A: Two large waterfalls on the border with the USA between Lake Erie and Lake Ontario attracting over 12 million visitors each year. Several people have crossed the falls on a tightrope!

Q: What is Nunavut?

A: Nunavut is the newest of the Canadian territories; it is also the largest. In 1999 it was separated from the Northwest Territories. It has only 30,000 inhabitants spread over an area the size of Greenland.

Wheat (right) is the most important single crop, and the Prairie provinces of Alberta, Manitoba, and Saskatchewan form one of the greatest wheat-growing areas of the world, each year producing more than 90% of Canadian wheat.

DATA BANK

Longest river
Mackenzie 2,635 miles (4,241 km)

Highest mountain
Mount Logan 19,551 ft (5,959 m)

Coastline
125,567 miles (202,080 km)

Climate
From more than 980 inches (2,500 cm) of rain and snow in the coastal range of the west to less than 10 inches (25 cm) on the Arctic coast. Winters are below freezing, long and severe in the centre and north. Summers are mild.

Largest city and population
Toronto (Ontario) 12,536,031

Annual income
US $34,000 or £19,000 approx. per person.

65

The United States of Am

The USA stretches from the Arctic Ocean to tropical Hawaii and includes the massive Rocky Mountains as well as fertile lowlands. Vast natural resources and a culture of enterprise make the USA one of the world's richest nations, the home of many global businesses

In the 1960s there was a race between the Soviet Union and the USA to land men on the moon. On July 20th 1969 USA's Apollo 11 made the first ever moon landing and this was followed by many others. Space exploration continued with the Space Shuttle flights, which take off from Cape Canaveral,

Stars: = 50 states
Stripes: = 13 colonys

Longest river
Mississippi 2,339 miles (3,765 km)

Highest mountain
Mount McKinley (Alaska)
20,322 ft (6,194 m)

Coastline
12,380 miles (19,924 km)

Climate
Wettest in the western mountains and Hawaii. Hottest in the south

Largest city and population
New York City 8,000,000

Annual income
US $41,800 or £24,000 approx. per person

Q&A

Q: What do the stars and stripes mean on the United States flag?

A: The flag of the United States has 13 horizontal red and white stripes, which represent the 13 original colonies. In the top left corner of the flag is a blue rectangle with 50 small, white stars. These represent the 50 states in the United States of America. The flag is known as 'the Stars and Stripes'.

Q: Did the *Mayflower* take the first settlers to America?

A: No. The first settlers are thought to have been a group of English traders who landed in Virginia in 1607. But the *Mayflower*, which sailed in 1620, is probably the most famous of the early ships to go to America. Those on board included 102 passengers from Holland and Britain. A replica of the *Mayflower* can be seen at Plymouth, Massachusetts (right).

Washington, the capital of the USA, was designed in 1791 by a French architect and was the world's first planned capital. Home to the White House (left) and government buildings, Washington, D.C. is one of America's most visited sites.

Fascinating Facts

The USA is the world leader in terms of earnings from international tourism. Tourists come from all over the world to see the natural beauty of the Rockies and the deserts, visit the great theme parks, and cities such as San Francisco, Las Vegas and New York.

There are over 500 recognised Native American tribes in the United States. They have the right to form their own government and to enforce their own laws. They do not have the power to make war or coin their own money.

The world's largest silver nugget, weighing 1,840 lb (835 kg) was found in 1894 near Aspen, Colorado.

Western USA

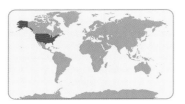

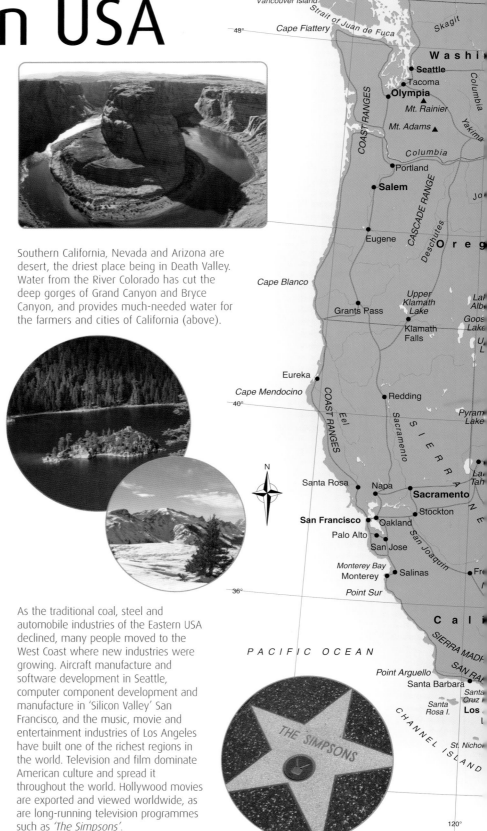

The Western USA contains the nation's most dramatic landscapes, being almost totally occupied by the Rocky Mountains which form several ranges of large mountains. The largest and widest mountains stretch 1,056 miles (1,700 km) from San Francisco through Utah to Denver, with many peaks over 9,842 ft (3,000 m) – the highest being Mount. Whitney at 14,505 ft (4,421 m). Vast quantities of powder snow make this one of the world's biggest winter skiing areas, the main centres being near Aspen in Colorado and Lake Tahoe in California (right).

Southern California, Nevada and Arizona are desert, the driest place being in Death Valley. Water from the River Colorado has cut the deep gorges of Grand Canyon and Bryce Canyon, and provides much-needed water for the farmers and cities of California (above).

Q&A

Q: Can animals and birds survive in the Great Salt Lake in Utah?

A: Yes. Although it is known as 'Utah's Dead Sea' the lake provides habitat for millions of shorebirds and waterfowl, including the beautiful pink flamingo.

Q: Does Washington State have any connection to Washington D.C.?

A: No. Washington is a state in the Pacific Northwest of the United States. The state is named after George Washington, the first President of the United States. It should not be confused with Washington, D.C., the nation's capital city. To avoid confusion' the state is often called Washington State, and the city of Washington D.C. is often called simply D.C.

As the traditional coal, steel and automobile industries of the Eastern USA declined, many people moved to the West Coast where new industries were growing. Aircraft manufacture and software development in Seattle, computer component development and manufacture in 'Silicon Valley' San Francisco, and the music, movie and entertainment industries of Los Angeles have built one of the richest regions in the world. Television and film dominate American culture and spread it throughout the world. Hollywood movies are exported and viewed worldwide, as are long-running television programmes such as 'The Simpsons'.

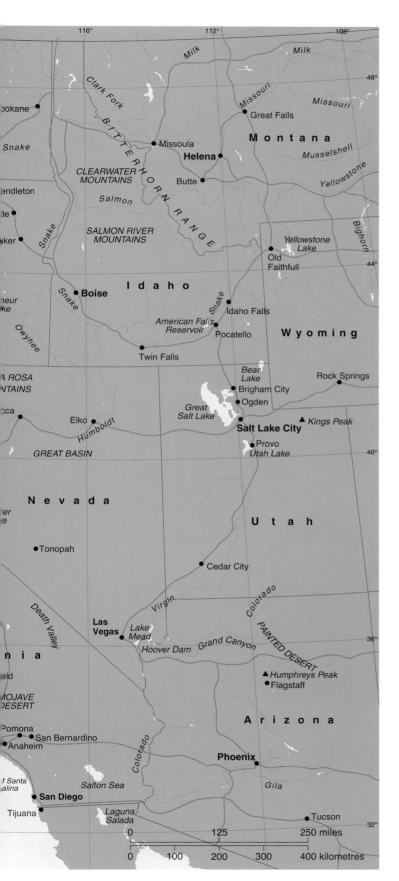

116° 112° 108°

Milk Milk

Clark Fork

•pokane

Snake Missoula
• Great Falls

Helena

M o n t a n a

CLEARWATER
MOUNTAINS Butte
Musselshell

endleton
Salmon Yellowstone

ade
SALMON RIVER
MOUNTAINS
Bighorn

uker Snake
Yellowstone
Lake
48°

Old
Faithfull 44°

• Boise **I d a h o**
Snake
Idaho Falls

meur American Falls
Reservoir Pocatello

ke
W y o m i n g

Owyhee Twin Falls

A ROSA
NTAINS Bear
Lake

Brigham City Rock Springs

cca Elko Great
Salt Lake Ogden

Humboldt ▲ Kings Peak
Salt Lake City
40°

GREAT BASIN Provo
Utah Lake

N e v a d a **U t a h**

•Tonopah

• Cedar City

Colorado
Virgin

ter Las
Death Valley **Vegas** Lake
Mead Grand Canyon 36°

nia Hoover Dam
PAINTED DESERT

eld ▲ Humphreys Peak
•Flagstaff

MOJAVE
DESERT

Pomona **A r i z o n a**
San Bernardino
Anaheim Colorado

Phoenix

f Santa Salton Sea Gila
alina
San Diego

Tijuana Laguna
Salada • Tucson 32°

0 125 250 miles

0 100 200 300 400 kilometres

DATA BANK

Population
68,197,932

Most heavily populated state
California, 33,871,648

Least heavily populated state
Wyoming, 493,782

Largest state by area
California
158,302 sq miles (410,000 sq km)
Width 250 miles (400 km), length
770 miles (1,240 km)

Smallest state by area
Hawaii 10,941 sq miles
(28,337 sq km) – 18 islands and atolls
stretch across a distance of 1,522
miles (2,450 km)

Highest point
Mount Whitney, California
14,505 ft (4421 m)

The Rocky Mountains
known as the Rockies
?(right), were formed by
the collision of two of
the earth's tectonic
plates, and earthquakes
are common.

Fascinating Facts

If California were its own country, it would have the
eighth largest economy in the world.

The world record for a single snowstorm is
190 inches (480 cm) at Mount Shasta Ski Bowl,
California, USA, between February 13 and 19, 1959.

In the 1800s a cowboy was the farm hand who
looked after beef cattle. Cowboys had to learn many
skills which were celebrated in festivals called rodeos.
These continue today with bareback riding, steer
wrestling, barrel racing, saddle bronco riding, team
roping, tie-down roping and bull riding?(below).

Eastern USA

Europeans have settled the Eastern half of the USA since 1613. People who migrated to settle permanently in colonies were called 'colonists' or 'settlers'. Sometimes the settlers formed the colony themselves if they settled in an unpopulated area. The word 'colony' comes from the Latin word 'colonus', meaning someone who works the land.

The Statue of Liberty, New York

Washington D.C., named after President George Washington, is the capital city, and home to the President of the United States, and to the Senate buildings (above).

The native tribe of the Manahattoes were the original inhabitants of New York. In 1613 the Dutch gave the name New Amsterdam to their settlement on Manhatten Island. In 1664, the British conquered the area and renamed it New York. The city grew, as it was the port at which all European settlers arrived.

Wall Street?(below), named after a wall the Dutch built to keep the British out, is now the world's major financial centre.

New Orleans, called the "Big Easy," due to its relaxed life-style, is the world's jazz capital, and the Mardis Gras festival attracts millions of visitors. In August 2005, Hurricane Katrina, the largest hurricane ever recorded over the USA, flooded over 80% of New Orleans. Over 1 million people were evacuated, 1,300 died, and the rebuilding costs will be billions of dollars.

Q&A

Q: Hurricanes are common in the Eastern USA, why do they have names?

A: It's less confusing to talk about storms, and warn people about the dangerous ones, if each one has a name. In 1953 the US Weather Bureau called all hurricanes by women's names, but in 1979, to avoid there being any criticism, men's names were added to the list.

Q: Peanuts are common in the Eastern USA. Are peanuts the same as monkey nuts?

A: Peanuts are also known as earth nuts, jack nuts, manila nuts and monkey nuts (although monkey nuts usually means the whole pod, not just the nut). Most of the peanuts grown in America are used to make peanut butter.

Large coal and iron ore deposits helped the rapid development of industries such as steel, automobiles, shipbuilding and textiles, and the rise of northern cities such as Chicago, Detroit, Pittsburgh and New York. The Southern States were initially more prosperous, having large tobacco and cotton plantations. However, this wealth depended on cheap slave labour.

Fascinating Facts

Disney World, near Orlando, Florida is the world's largest tourist attraction, covering an area of 30,000 acres (12,140 hectares).

New London, Connecticut, is 355 years old, but its name is only 343 years old. It took more than ten years to agree to the name.

The windiest place in the world is Mount Washington, New Hampshire, where a surface wind speed of 230 mph (370 km/h) was recorded on April 12, 1934.

DATA BANK

Population
238,547,698

Most heavily populated state
Texas, 20,851,820

Least heavily populated state
Vermont, 608,827

Largest state by area
Texas, 267,338 sq miles
(692,405 sq km)

Smallest state by area
Rhode Island, 1,214 sq miles
(3,144 sq km)

Highest point
Texas, Guadalupe Peak, 8,751 ft
(2,667 m)

Mexico

Mexico, its capital city, and population:

| Mexico | Mexico (District) | 107,449,525 |

Mexico borders the USA to the north and Guatemala to the south and has two high, coastal mountain ranges, between which is a high plateau, or 'altiplano'. Once home to the Aztec and Mayan cultures, the Spanish conquistadors (soldiers and explorers) came to plunder gold and silver in the 16th century, and so Mexico is the world's largest Spanish-speaking nation. Only 15% of the land is farmed, the rest being mountain or desert, making the rural areas very poor. Industry thrives along the US border where US companies take advantage of the low labour costs. Tourism is increasing at both the tropical beaches and the Aztec and Mayan archaeological sites.

Another name for Aztecs was Mexica, from which the country takes its modern name. The Aztecs were very wealthy because they were able to trade gold and silver. Spanish explorers were amazed at the treasures of the Aztecs and came to Mexico with soldiers to steal it for themselves.

Lacking metal swords, the Aztecs were no match for Herman Cortez and his Spanish soldiers and they were defeated in 1521, as the colonization of this wealthy land began. The Spanish conquistadors quickly expanded their search for hidden treasures and found massive silver deposits. Mines were built, the native peoples were enslaved and forced into hard labour, and the treasure was sent back to Spain. News of this lucrative new land spread quickly; colonists arrived by the hundreds of thousands in search of personal riches.

Fascinating Facts

The Mayans (ancient Mexicans) enjoyed chewing on chicle, the sap of the sapodilla tree?(right). This Central American tree resin was the basis for modern chewing gum.

Many scientists believe that a large comet hit the Yucatan peninsula 65 million years ago, causing dramatic changes to the climate, and leading to the extinction of the dinosaurs.

Maize, one of the world's major grain crops, was cultivated in Mexico many thousands of years ago. Maize was sacred to the Aztecs and maize gods were worshipped.

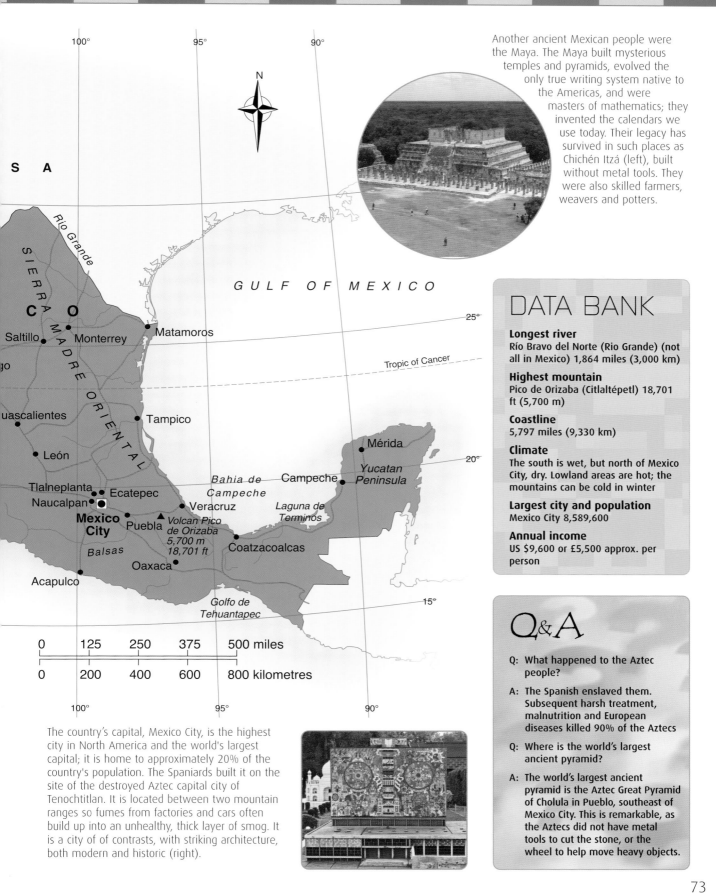

100° 95° 90°

N

Another ancient Mexican people were the Maya. The Maya built mysterious temples and pyramids, evolved the only true writing system native to the Americas, and were masters of mathematics; they invented the calendars we use today. Their legacy has survived in such places as Chichén Itzá (left), built without metal tools. They were also skilled farmers, weavers and potters.

S A

Río Grande

SIERRA MADRE ORIENTAL

C O

GULF OF MEXICO

25°

Saltillo

Monterrey

Matamoros

Tropic of Cancer

go

uascalientes

Tampico

León

Mérida

20°

Bahía de Campeche

Campeche

Yucatan Peninsula

Tlalneplanta

Ecatepec

Naucalpan

Veracruz

Mexico City

Puebla

▲ Volcan Pico de Orizaba 5,700 m 18,701 ft

Laguna de Terminos

Coatzacoalcas

Balsas

Oaxaca

Acapulco

Golfo de Tehuantapec

15°

0	125	250	375	500 miles
0	200	400	600	800 kilometres

100° 95° 90°

DATA BANK

Longest river
Río Bravo del Norte (Rio Grande) (not all in Mexico) 1,864 miles (3,000 km)

Highest mountain
Pico de Orizaba (Citlaltépetl) 18,701 ft (5,700 m)

Coastline
5,797 miles (9,330 km)

Climate
The south is wet, but north of Mexico City, dry. Lowland areas are hot; the mountains can be cold in winter

Largest city and population
Mexico City 8,589,600

Annual income
US $9,600 or £5,500 approx. per person

Q&A

Q: What happened to the Aztec people?

A: The Spanish enslaved them. Subsequent harsh treatment, malnutrition and European diseases killed 90% of the Aztecs

Q: Where is the world's largest ancient pyramid?

A: The world's largest ancient pyramid is the Aztec Great Pyramid of Cholula in Pueblo, southeast of Mexico City. This is remarkable, as the Aztecs did not have metal tools to cut the stone, or the wheel to help move heavy objects.

The country's capital, Mexico City, is the highest city in North America and the world's largest capital; it is home to approximately 20% of the country's population. The Spaniards built it on the site of the destroyed Aztec capital city of Tenochtitlan. It is located between two mountain ranges so fumes from factories and cars often build up into an unhealthy, thick layer of smog. It is a city of of contrasts, with striking architecture, both modern and historic (right).

73

Central and South America

BELIZE
GUATEMALA ● Belmopan
HONDURAS
Guatemala City ● ● Tegucig
EL SALVADOR ● NICARAGUA
San Salvador ● ● Managu
COSTA RICA ● Pan
San José ● PANA
Panama canal

NORTH PACIFIC OCEAN

Quib

Galápagos Is
(Ecuador)

Qui

ECUAD

L

SOUTH PACIFIC OCEAN

S tretching from the tropical forests of Venezuela to just a short distance from Antarctica, South America is a continent of contrasts. The Andes Mountains stretch the length of the western side of the continent. The Amazon Basin, the part of South America drained by the Amazon River and its tributaries, holds over 60% of all the flowing water in the world.

The people of South America originally came across the Bering Strait (above) in the Arctic Ocean from Asia during the last ice age, which ended 10,000 years ago. Anthropologists believe that groups of people crossed to North America, and over countless generations, made their way down to Central America and into South America. (An anthropologist is someone who studies human beings, particularly the cultures of ancient civilisations. It was a science developed in the 18th century, when scientists first studied how people lived and how the human race developed.)

Then, 500 years ago, the Spanish and Portuguese conquered the land, and the main languages are now Portuguese (in Brazil) and Spanish (in Argentina). (Argentina means 'land of silver' in Spanish.) This changed the lives and cultures of the native peoples of the continent. Their populations were destroyed by displacement (being removed from their homes), by disease, and by warfare and enslavement.

Today, the people of South America represent hundreds of culturally distinct nations and tribes (above right and far right). Many were nomadic or semi-nomadic, others lived in permanent villages and built up farming communities, while others created large-scale cities. These people included the Maya, Aztec, Inca, Cahokia and many others.

Fascinating Facts

The tomato is a native South American plant; its name comes from the Aztec language.

Lake Nicaragua in Nicaragua is the only freshwater lake in the world that has sharks.

One of the largest street carnivals in the world is held every February in Rio de Janerio, Brazil.

The Inca city of Machu Pichu in Peru, which was built high in the Peruvian Andes, was not discovered until 1911. It is now a very popular tourist attraction.

0	300	600	900	1200 miles
0	500	1000	1500	2000 kilometres

Q&A

Q: What is the Altiplano?

A: Altiplano is the Spanish word for high plain or plateau (left). In Southern America the Altiplano is an area in the Central Andes, running though Chile, Argentina, Bolivia and Peru. Corn and wheat are the principal crops here, and mining is the chief industry.

Q: How long is the Panama Canal?

A: The Panama Canal, located in Panama, is 51 miles (82 km) long. Once the canal was opened, in 1914, ships no longer had to travel all the way to the southern tip of South America and around the dangerous seas off Cape Horn.

Caracas

VENEZUELA

Georgetown
Paramaribo

GUYANA

SURINAME

Cayenne

FRENCH
GUIANA

MBIA

Amazon

B R A Z I L

La Paz

B O L I V I A

Brazilia

PARAGUAY

Rio de
Janeiro

São Paulo

Rivadavia

Asunción

URUGUAY

Buenos
Aires

Montevideo

A R G E N T I N A

Sarmiento

*SOUTH
ATLANTIC
OCEAN*

*Falkland Is
(UK)*

The Amazonian piranha (below) is a vicious killer fish. Attacks are swift and comprehensive, as they will start eating their victim alive. Their razor-sharp teeth interlock, and natives of South America use them to make tools and weapons.

DATA BANK

Longest river
Amazon (Brazil, Peru, Bolivia, Colombia, Ecuador, Venezuela) 3,969 miles (6,387 km)

Highest mountain
Mount Aconcagua (Argentina) 22,831 ft (6,959 m)

Climate
Varies from the hot and dry in Mexico, through tropical Brazil to the arid south.

Natural resources
Aluminium, copper, nickel, oil, silver

Population
517,300,324

Richest / poorest country
Argentina is the richest country per head of population and Bolivia is the poorest.

About Central and South America

The countries of Central and South America, their capital cities and population:

Argentina	Buenos Aires	39,921,833
Belize	Belmopan	287,730
Bolivia	La Paz (seat of gov)	
	Sucre (legal capital)	8,989,046
Brazil	Brasilia	186,112,794
Chile	Santiago	16,134,219
Colombia	Bogota	43,593,035
Costa Rica	San José	4,075,261
Ecuador	Quito	13,547,510
El Salvador	San Salvador	6,822,378
Guatemala	Guatemala	12,293,545
Guyana	Georgetown	767,245
Honduras	Tegucigalpa	7,326,496
Nicaragua	Managua	5,570,129
Panama	Panama City	3,039,150
Paraguay	Asuncion	6,506,464
Peru	Lima	28,302,603
Suriname	Paramaribo	438,144
Uruguay	Montevideo	3,431,932
Venezuela	Caracas	25,730,435

Famous People

- Atahuallpa (1502–33) Last ruler of the Incas was captured by the Spanish after a five-year struggle and was executed.

- Eva Perón (1919–52) Eva Perón was the wife of the Argentinean President, Juan Perón. Fondly known as 'Evita' she became immensely popular. Her early death turned her into a cultural icon.

- Pelé (b. 1940). Full name: Edson Arantes do Nascimento. Famous Brazilian-born football player. He is the only person to have played in four world cup competitions (below).

Languages

- Spanish and Portuguese are the main languages of Central and Southern America. Portuguese speakers are called Lusophones (this comes from the word Lusitania, the Latin name for Portugal).

- Many other languages are used in this region by small groups of people – most of these will also speak Spanish and Portuguese. Aymará is spoken in Bolivia and Peru, Quechua in Bolivia, Peru and Ecuador, and also in parts of Chile and Argentina. English is spoken in Guyana and Belize, Guarani in Paraguay, and Mapudungun in parts of Chile and Argentina. Hindi, Dutch and Indonesian are spoken in Suriname, and Italian in Argentina, Brazil and Uruguay. German is spoken in Argentina, Brazil, Chile and Paraguay. Welsh is spoken in Patagonia, an area of Argentina.

Natural features

- The Andes is the world's longest mountain range. It forms a continuous chain, of over 4,350 miles (7,000 km) of high land from north to south of South America. In places it is 310 miles (500 km) wide, and reaches a height of some 13,100 ft (4,000 m).

- The Atacama Desert is sandwiched between the Pacific and the Andes in northern Chile. It is the driest place on earth.

- The Amazon River is the second longest river in the world. It is 3,969 miles (6,387 km) long and between 1 and 6 miles (1.6–9.5 km) wide.

- The Amazon rainforest stretched east from the Andes and is the largest rainforest on Earth. It is home to a huge variety of plants and animals, including 2.5 million insect species!

Natural resources

- Copper is mined in Chile and in Peru.
- Aluminium is mined in Venezuela and Brazil.
- Nickel is mined in Brazil.
- Oil is found in Venezuela and in Colombia.

Land use

- The vast Amazon rainforest is exploited for its timber and is being cleared for agricultural use. As the area diminishes, the animals and birds lose their habitat.

- The Pampas, meaning plain or flatlands, are the fertile lowlands of Argentina. The climate is mild, and the area is used for rearing cattle and for growing wheat.
- The Panama Canal was cut through Panama at the narrowest point of Central America to ease the journey from the Atlantic to the Pacific. To enable the ships to negotiate the uneven terrain, a series of locks are used.
- Farmers in the valleys of Bolivia produce barley, corn, wheat, fruits, and vegetables. They export crops such as tea and coffee. However, the farmers in the valleys suffer great isolation and the lack of direct access to markets.
- In the 1970s and 1980s, as a direct response to international demand, Paraguayan farmers have increased their production of soya beans and cotton. Today 40% of land has been put aside for these products. 60% of the crop is for export, thus boosting the country's economy.
- Belize is a tiny country, whose economy is based primarily on agriculture and tourism – (it is a popular place for scuba diving). Sugar, citrus fruits and bananas are the main crops, accounting for over half of all exports.

- Chile is a long and narrow coastal country, over 2,880 miles (4,630 km) north to south, but only 265 miles (430 km) at its widest point east to west. The northern Atacama Desert contains great mineral wealth, primarily copper. A large proportion of Chile's income is from the copper mining industry.

Industry

- Brazil has a large industrial base and is the most developed of the South American countries.

- Brazil produces 25% of the world's coffee and is self-sufficient in food, and exports quantities of sugar cane, soya beans, cotton and oranges.
- Argentina grows wheat and has a large beef exporting industry.
- The rich soil of the central region allows Chile to produce world-renowned wines.
- Paraguay is able to produce all its own electricity and still have some to spare for export from one giant hydroelectric dam on the Paraná River: the Itaipú Dam.

Environment

- Central and Southern America are comparatively free of industrial pollution but there is a major problem with excessive deforestation of the Amazon rainforest. This is causing soil erosion and added pressure on global warming, as there are fewer trees to convert carbon dioxide into oxygen.

- The countries of Central America are rich in plant and animal life. Around 7% of the world's animal species live in the forests and beaches of this region. The population of Central America is approximately 37 million, with a yearly growth rate of about 3%. Expanding economies and growing populations have caused the environmental quality of the region to decline. The fear is that some plants and animals may disappear.
- Over the last 100 years Costa Rica has lost around 60% if its rainforest. The reason for this is the increasing demand from around the world for bananas. The countries of Central and Southern America are among the highest banana producers. An added environmental issue alongside the destruction of the rainforest is how to properly dispose of the blue plastic bags which are used to protect the bananas from insects and bad weather. These could have a devastating effect on the wildlife if not disposed of carefully.

Africa

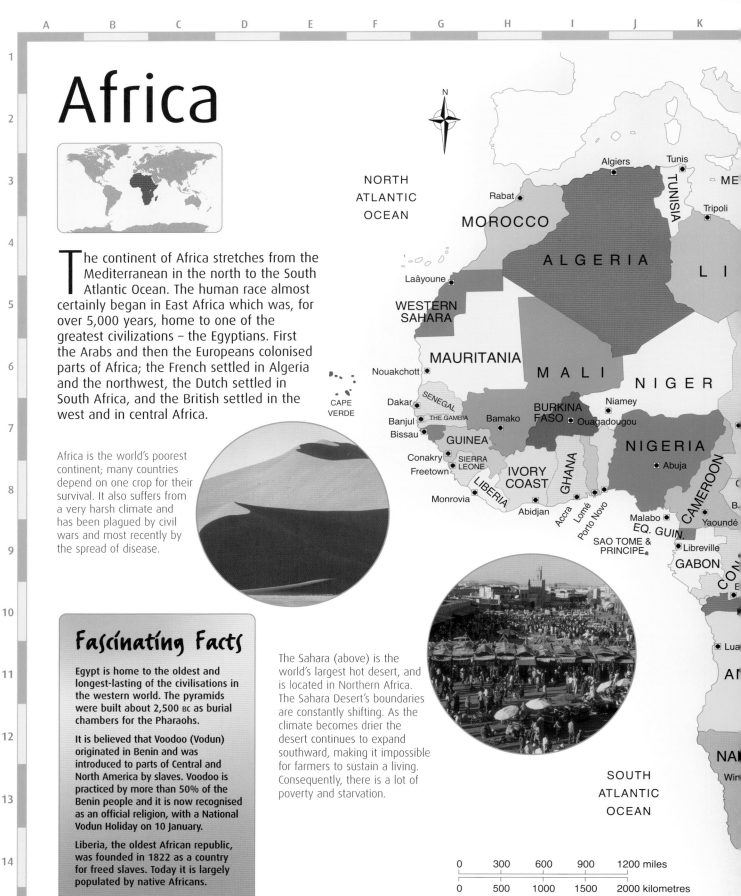

The continent of Africa stretches from the Mediterranean in the north to the South Atlantic Ocean. The human race almost certainly began in East Africa which was, for over 5,000 years, home to one of the greatest civilizations – the Egyptians. First the Arabs and then the Europeans colonised parts of Africa; the French settled in Algeria and the northwest, the Dutch settled in South Africa, and the British settled in the west and in central Africa.

Africa is the world's poorest continent; many countries depend on one crop for their survival. It also suffers from a very harsh climate and has been plagued by civil wars and most recently by the spread of disease.

Fascinating Facts

Egypt is home to the oldest and longest-lasting of the civilisations in the western world. The pyramids were built about 2,500 BC as burial chambers for the Pharaohs.

It is believed that Voodoo (Vodun) originated in Benin and was introduced to parts of Central and North America by slaves. Voodoo is practiced by more than 50% of the Benin people and it is now recognised as an official religion, with a National Vodun Holiday on 10 January.

Liberia, the oldest African republic, was founded in 1822 as a country for freed slaves. Today it is largely populated by native Africans.

The Sahara (above) is the world's largest hot desert, and is located in Northern Africa. The Sahara Desert's boundaries are constantly shifting. As the climate becomes drier the desert continues to expand southward, making it impossible for farmers to sustain a living. Consequently, there is a lot of poverty and starvation.

NORTH ATLANTIC OCEAN

Algiers
Tunis
TUNISIA
ME
Rabat
Tripoli
MOROCCO
ALGERIA
LI
Laâyoune
WESTERN SAHARA
MAURITANIA
MALI
NIGER
Nouakchott
Niamey
Dakar
SENEGAL
Banjul
THE GAMBIA
Bamako
BURKINA FASO
Ouagadougou
Bissau
GUINEA
NIGERIA
Conakry
SIERRA LEONE
Abuja
Freetown
IVORY COAST
GHANA
CAMEROON
LIBERIA
Monrovia
Abidjan
Accra
Lomé
Porto Novo
Malabo
EQ. GUIN.
Yaoundé
B.
SAO TOME & PRINCIPE
Libreville
GABON
CON
E
Lua
AN
NA
Win
SOUTH ATLANTIC OCEAN

CAPE VERDE

0	300	600	900	1200 miles
0	500	1000	1500	2000 kilometres

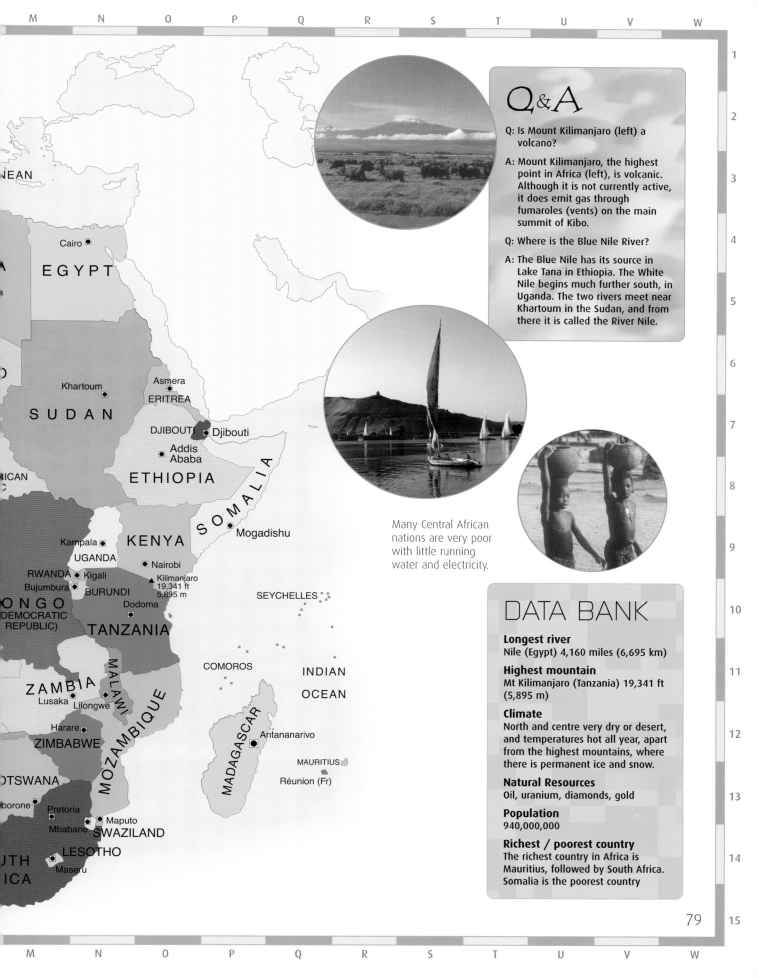

Q&A

Q: Is Mount Kilimanjaro (left) a volcano?

A: Mount Kilimanjaro, the highest point in Africa (left), is volcanic. Although it is not currently active, it does emit gas through fumaroles (vents) on the main summit of Kibo.

Q: Where is the Blue Nile River?

A: The Blue Nile has its source in Lake Tana in Ethiopia. The White Nile begins much further south, in Uganda. The two rivers meet near Khartoum in the Sudan, and from there it is called the River Nile.

Many Central African nations are very poor with little running water and electricity.

DATA BANK

Longest river
Nile (Egypt) 4,160 miles (6,695 km)

Highest mountain
Mt Kilimanjaro (Tanzania) 19,341 ft (5,895 m)

Climate
North and centre very dry or desert, and temperatures hot all year, apart from the highest mountains, where there is permanent ice and snow.

Natural Resources
Oil, uranium, diamonds, gold

Population
940,000,000

Richest / poorest country
The richest country in Africa is Mauritius, followed by South Africa. Somalia is the poorest country

Map labels: NEAN · Cairo · EGYPT · Khartoum · SUDAN · Asmera · ERITREA · DJIBOUTI · Djibouti · Addis Ababa · ETHIOPIA · SOMALIA · AFRICAN · Kampala · UGANDA · KENYA · Nairobi · Mogadishu · RWANDA · Kigali · Bujumbura · BURUNDI · Kilimanjaro 19,341 ft 5,895 m · ONGO (DEMOCRATIC REPUBLIC) · Dodoma · TANZANIA · SEYCHELLES · COMOROS · INDIAN OCEAN · ZAMBIA · MALAWI · Lusaka · Lilongwe · MOZAMBIQUE · Harare · ZIMBABWE · MADAGASCAR · Antananarivo · MAURITIUS · Réunion (Fr) · OTSWANA · borone · Pretoria · Maputo · Mbabane · SWAZILAND · LESOTHO · UTH ICA · Maseru

About Africa

The countries of Africa, their capital cities and population:

Country	Capital	Population
Algeria	Algiers	32,531,853
Angola	Luanda	12,366,031
Benin	Porto-Novo	7,460,025
Botswana	Gaborone	1,448,454
Burkina Faso	Ouagadougou	12,266,293
Burundi	Bujumbura	5,537.387
Cameroon	Yaounde	15,029,433
Cape Verde	Praia	399,857
Central African Republic	Bangu	3,375,771
Chad	N'Djamena	9,359,512
Comoros	Moroni	545,528
Congo, Democratic Republic of	Kinshasa	62,660,551
Congo, Republic of	Brazzaville	2,658,123
Cote d'Ivoire	Yamoussoukro	15,446,231
Djibouti	Djibouti	440,727
Egypt	Cairo	77,050,004
Equatorial Guinea	Malabo	454,001
Eritrea	Asmara	3,842,436
Ethiopia	Addis Ababa	58,390,351
Gabon	Libreville	1,207,844
Gambia	Banjul	1,291,858
Ghana	Accra	18,497,206
Guinea	Conakry	9,447,110
Guinea-Bissau	Bissau	1,206,311
Kenya	Nairobi	21,443,636
Lesotho	Maseru	2,089,829
Liberia	Monrovia	2,771,901
Libya	Tripoli	5,690,727
Madagascar	Antananarivo	14,462,509
Malawi	Lilongwe	9,840,474
Mali	Bamako	10,108,569
Mauritania	Nouakchott	2,511,473
Mauritius	Port Louis	1,168,256
Morocco	Rabat	29,114,497
Mozambique	Maputo	18,641,460
Namibia	Windhoek	1,622,328
Niger	Niamey	9,671,848
Nigeria	Abuja	110,532,242
Rwanda	Kigali	7,956,172
São Tomé & Principe	São Tomé	150,123
Senegal	Dakar	9,723,149
Seychelles	Victoria	78,641
Sierra Leone	Freetown	5,080,004
Somalia	Mogadishu	6,841,695
South Africa	Pretoria	43,986,918
Sudan	Khartoum	40,550,552
Swaziland	Mbabane	996,462
Tanzania	Dar es Salaam	37,608,769
Togo	Lome	4,905,827
Tunisia	Tunis	9,380,404
Uganda	Kampala	27,200,000
Western Sahara	El Aaiun	273,008
Zambia	Lusaka	11,460,736
Zimbabwe	Harare	11,044,147

Famous people

- Nelson Mandela (born 1918). One of the leaders of the African resistance to the South African Apartheid regime. Apartheid means racial separation, that is, keeping different races apart. After spending 25 years in prison on Robben Island he became the first President of the New South African Republic. He is a revered world statesman and was awarded the Nobel Peace Prize in 1993.

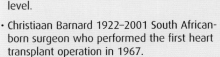

- Haile Gebrselassie (born 1973) is a long distance runner from Ethiopia?(right). He is considered to be one of the best distance runners of all time. His talent may be connected to the fact that he is from Asella in the Arsi Province, which is 8,000 ft (2,440 m) above sea level.

- Christiaan Barnard 1922–2001 South African-born surgeon who performed the first heart transplant operation in 1967.

- Cleopatra (below). The last Egyptian queen. She was immortalised in Shakespeare's play, Anthony and Cleopatra.

Natural resources

- Oil is found in Libya, Algeria and Nigeria, Sierra Leone, Liberia and Ghana.

- Uranium is mined in Niger and Angola.

- Diamonds are found in South Africa, Botswana and Democratic Republic of Congo.

- Gold is mined in South Africa, Zambia, Ghana.

Borders

- Before the colonisation of Africa in the 19th century there were no rigid national borders, as the population was largely nomadic. Borders were created to separate the territories of the different European groups. That's why there are so many straight lines on a political map. As the nations gained independence during the 1950s and 60s these borders remained and have been the source of some problems as they do not necessarily match the natural ethnic make-up of the people who live within them.

Industry

- Tea plantations: Kenya is the third largest producer of tea in the world, and is a major source of the country's income. Tea is grown mainly in the Kenyan Highlands, west of the Rift Valley, at altitudes of between 4,921–5,741 ft (1,500–1,750 m). Tea exports raise around $350 million (£220 million) each year.

- Agriculture: many parts of Africa are very fertile. Vast farms like this one below are found in the Western Cape.

- Wine from South Africa has also become very popular.

- Diamond mining: South Africa is one of the leading diamond producing nations. Johannesburg is one of the largest centres for the gold and diamond trade, due to its location on the mineral rich Witwatersrand range of hills.

- Tourism: the abundant wild life on the game reserves is a huge attraction, as is the Kenyan and South African coast.

Languages

Africa is home to as many as a thousand languages, the best known being Shona, Swahili, Yoruba and Zulu. They fall into four main groups according to the area where they are spoken. They are:

- The Afro – Asiatic languages of east and north Africa.

- The Nilo – Saharan languages spoken in countries from Chad to Tanzania.

- The Niger – Congo languages, which is the largest group and is spoken in large areas of sub-Saharan Africa.

- The Khoisan languages, that are used in southern Africa.

European languages were introduced as the various European countries colonised Africa in the 19th century. The main settlers were British, French, Belgian, Portuguese and Dutch.

Natural features

- The fertile Nile Delta (a delta is the area where a river flows into the sea or a lake – often called the mouth of a river) is home to the densest population in Africa, i.e. Cairo and Alexandria. Cairo has a population of 7,734,614 and 3,811,516 people live in Alexandria.

- Great Rift Valley: two tectonic plates which have separated and formed this great valley which extends from Tanzania in the south, through the whole of Kenya and into Ethiopia in the North. It is still susceptible to earthquakes.

- Sahara Desert, the largest desert in the world. Many of the inhabitants of the Sahara are nomadic, that is, they move from place to place in communities rather than settling in one place. One reason for not staying in one place is so that their animals will have sufficient food, as the pasture becomes depleted rapidly in the desert areas.

Culture

- Africa is home to many tribes and ethnic groups. Some groups represent populations consisting of millions of people, others are smaller groups of a few thousand. All these tribes and groups have cultures which are different, but represent the mosaic of cultural diversity of Africa.

- African dances are an important method of communication, and dancers use gestures, masks, costumes, and body painting.

- Art and jewellery have an important place in Africa – using natural products such as shells or wood.

Environment

- Many parts of Africa have to live with soil erosion and deforestation. Cutting down large areas of trees is called deforestation. This eventually causes soil erosion; this means that the soil can be washed away by the rain or blown away by the wind. Mali uses 5.5 million tonnes of wood each year and this involves cutting down large areas of woodland; the woodlands will eventually disappear altogether.

- In Ethiopia, the land is also subject to soil erosion, drought, deforestation and overgrazing. Water shortages are common in the dry season.

- In Eritrea, as well as the conditions mentioned above, there is a serious land loss due to land mines. The Eritrean Government has begun a programme of reforestation and are attempting to dissuade the population from using wood as fuel.

North Africa

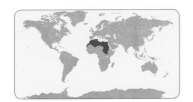

N orth Africa or northern Africa is the northernmost region of the African continent. It generally includes the following territories: Algeria, Chad, Egypt, Libya, Mali, Mauritania, Morocco, Niger, Sudan, Tunisia and the Western Sahara. Sometimes Algeria, Egypt, Libya, Morocco, Niger, Sudan, Tunisia are classed as the Middle East because, culturally, the people have close ties with that region.

Algeria, Libya and Tunisia are oil and gas-rich states bordering the Mediterranean Sea. Morocco borders the Atlantic Ocean, Egypt borders the Mediterranean and Red Seas, and Sudan occupies the Eastern Sahara. Much of Libya and Algeria are part of the Sahara desert, and there is little agriculture apart from that found in the fertile valleys of the Atlas Mountains and along the River Nile.

Fascinating Facts

The world's highest measured sand dunes are those in the Saharan sand sea of Algeria. They reach a height of 1,500 ft (460 m).

The River Nile is the world's longest river, it is 4,160 miles (6,695 km) long and starts south of the equator in Central Africa with over half its length crossing the Sahara Desert.

Date palms (right) are fruit trees, which can remain productive for over a hundred years. They have always been important in Morocco. It used to be unlawful to sell a tree, because it was a family's source of food.

The Western Sahara region was controlled by Spain until 1976 and is now claimed by Morocco, but fought over by desert tribesmen. The Berbers are the native people of the area. They were conquered over 1,000 years ago by the Arabs, and the region is still Islamic and Arabic speaking.

One of the world's most famous trade routes ran from Morocco (taking salt from the Mediterranean) through the Sahara to the market cities on the River Niger. Gold, slaves, ostrich feathers, spices and precious wood were carried back to the ports on the Atlantic coast.

When searching for oil in the southern deserts of Libya, vast underground resources of water were discovered, which are being tapped by the 'Great Manmade River Project', the world's largest civil engineering scheme. This will enable Libya to have fresh water in the coastal cities and to irrigate the desert. Libya hopes not only to grow its own food, but also to export it to Europe.

Q&A

Q: Why is the camel known as 'the ship of the desert'?

A: The camel is adapted to surviving in the desert. Its hump stores enough fat to keep it going for several weeks without food.

Q: Do crops grow in the desert areas?

A: On the desert fringes it's possible to grow olives, figs, dates and citrus fruits, as well as a variety of cereals, plus rice and cotton. However access to water is essential to improve crop yields.

The Sahara desert (left) is the largest in the world. The boundaries of the Sahara are constantly shifting. The whole region was wet and fertile only around 8,000 years ago. Since then the climate has become drier, and the desert continues to expand southwards. Underground water, flowing from the Atlas Mountains, comes to the surface at oases. The River Nile passes through the Sahara and transforms the sandy wastes into a lush, fertile plain.

DATA BANK

Longest river
Nile (Egypt) 4,160 miles (6,695 km)

Highest mountain
Jebel Toubkal (Morocco) 13,665 ft (4,165 m)

Coastline
4,483 miles (7,215 km)

Climate
Only the Atlas Mountains and the south of Sudan have significant rain. Very hot in the desert, although winter nights can be cold.

Largest city and population
Casablanca (Morocco) 3,344,300

Annual income
US $5,000 or £3,000 approx. per person

Egypt's great wealth was based on the water and fertile silt provided by the annual floods of the River Nile. Tourists and archaeologists from around the world visit Egypt to see the temples and pyramids between Aswan and Cairo.

Tutankhamen

Map labels

MEDITERRANEAN SEA
Tripoli
Misurata
Leptis Magna
Benghazi
Derna
Alexandria
Port Said
Suez Canal
Suez
Pyramids of Giza
Cairo
EGYPT
LIBYA
DESERT
Asyût
Nile
Qena
Valley of the Kings
Thebes
Aswân
Lake Nasser
RED SEA
Nubian Desert
Port Sudan
CHAD
SUDAN
Merowe
Atbara
Kassala
Khartoum
Lake Chad
Abéché
JABAL MARRAH
Geneina
Ndjamena
El Obeid
Kosti
Blue Nile
Atbara
White Nile
Bongor
Sarh
Nimule

West Africa

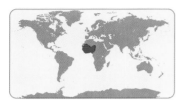

S tretching from the heart of the Sahara Desert to the tropical forests of southern Nigeria, this is one of the poorest areas of the world. The northern countries of Mali and Niger are plagued by drought, famine and the advancing Sahara, whilst the southern states of Sierra Leone, Liberia, Ghana and Nigeria are rich in oil.

Cocoa (right) originates from South America and was brought to Ghana in the late 19th century by Tetteh Quarshie who established the first cocoa farm. The Ghanaian cocoa industry grew in importance with Ghana becoming a major cocoa producer.

Fascinating Facts

The largest church in the world is the Basilica of Our Lady of Peace in Yamoussoukro, Côte d' Ivoire (Ivory Coast) with an area of 323,000 sq ft (30,000 sq m) and is 520 ft (158 m) high.

The Grand Mosque in Djenne, Mali, is the largest mud building in the world, measuring 330 ft (100 m) long and 130 ft (40 m) wide. For generations skilled craftsmen, the Baris, have maintained the architecture of the mosque, as well as the rest of the mud-built town, which tends to erode in the rainy season.

The Akosombo hydroelectric dam, built in 1964, created Lake Volta, one of the world's largest artificial lakes. It produces most of Ghana's electricity.

MAURITANIA
⊙ Nouakchott

Nouâdhibou

Sénégal

Dakar
⊙ SENEGAL

M A

Timbuktu

Ni

Banjul ⊙ GAMBIA

Bissau ⊙ GUINEA BISSAU

Bamako ⊙

BURKINO

Ouagad ⊙ FASO

Bobo Dioulasso ⊙

GUINEA

Conakry ⊙

SIERRA ⊙ LEONE
Freetown

IVORY COAST

GHANA

CO

LIBERIA

Lake Volta

Lon

Monrovia

Abidjan ⊡

Accra ⊡

| 0 | 150 | 300 | 450 | 600 miles |

| 0 | 200 | 400 | 600 | 800 | 1000 kilometres |

GULF O

Port Harcourt, on the Niger Delta, is the centre of Nigeria's oil industry. Oil provides 65% of Nigeria's income, but farm output has failed to keep pace with population increase, so the country must import food.

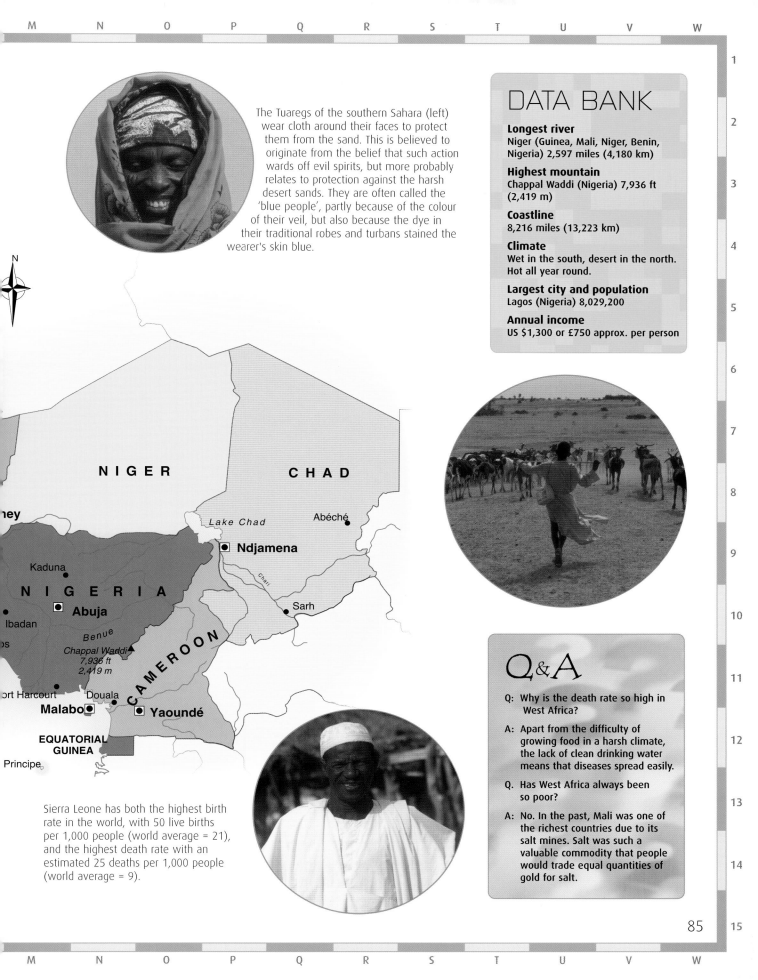

The Tuaregs of the southern Sahara (left) wear cloth around their faces to protect them from the sand. This is believed to originate from the belief that such action wards off evil spirits, but more probably relates to protection against the harsh desert sands. They are often called the 'blue people', partly because of the colour of their veil, but also because the dye in their traditional robes and turbans stained the wearer's skin blue.

DATA BANK

Longest river
Niger (Guinea, Mali, Niger, Benin, Nigeria) 2,597 miles (4,180 km)

Highest mountain
Chappal Waddi (Nigeria) 7,936 ft (2,419 m)

Coastline
8,216 miles (13,223 km)

Climate
Wet in the south, desert in the north. Hot all year round.

Largest city and population
Lagos (Nigeria) 8,029,200

Annual income
US $1,300 or £750 approx. per person

N I G E R

C H A D

Lake Chad

Abéché

⊙ **Ndjamena**

Chari

Kaduna

N I G E R I A

⊡ **Abuja**

Ibadan

Benue

▲Chappal Waddi
7,936 ft
2,419 m

Sarh

C A M E R O O N

rt Harcourt   Douala

Malabo⊡   ⊡ **Yaoundé**

**EQUATORIAL
GUINEA**

Principe

ey

os

N

Sierra Leone has both the highest birth rate in the world, with 50 live births per 1,000 people (world average = 21), and the highest death rate with an estimated 25 deaths per 1,000 people (world average = 9).

Q&A

Q: Why is the death rate so high in West Africa?

A: Apart from the difficulty of growing food in a harsh climate, the lack of clean drinking water means that diseases spread easily.

Q: Has West Africa always been so poor?

A: No. In the past, Mali was one of the richest countries due to its salt mines. Salt was such a valuable commodity that people would trade equal quantities of gold for salt.

Central Africa

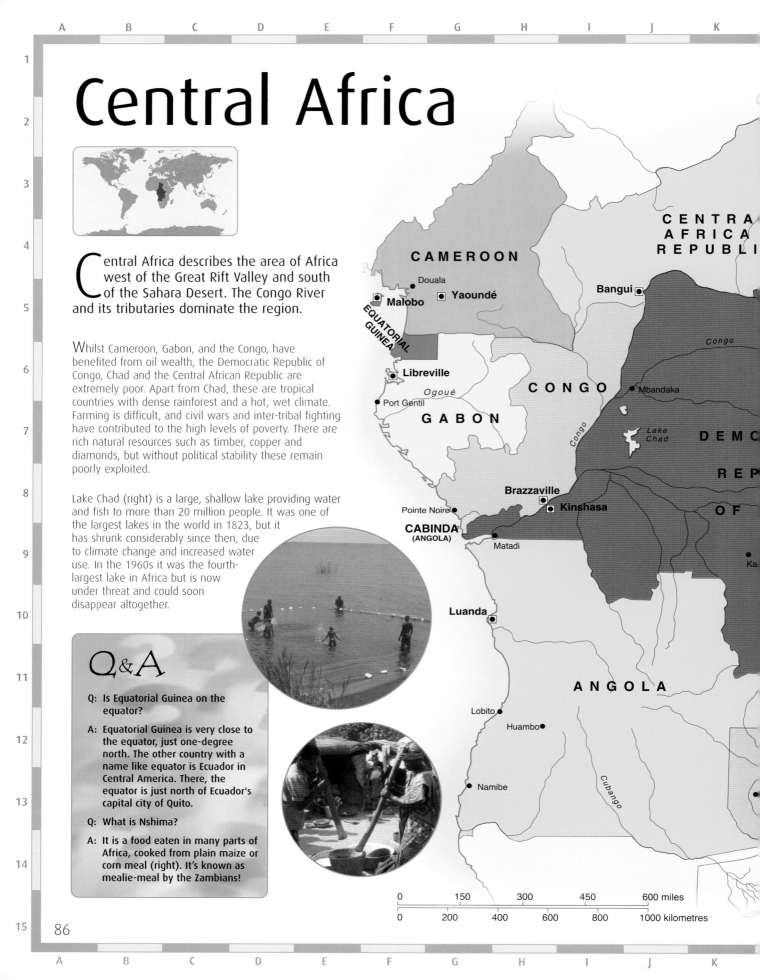

Central Africa describes the area of Africa west of the Great Rift Valley and south of the Sahara Desert. The Congo River and its tributaries dominate the region.

Whilst Cameroon, Gabon, and the Congo, have benefited from oil wealth, the Democratic Republic of Congo, Chad and the Central African Republic are extremely poor. Apart from Chad, these are tropical countries with dense rainforest and a hot, wet climate. Farming is difficult, and civil wars and inter-tribal fighting have contributed to the high levels of poverty. There are rich natural resources such as timber, copper and diamonds, but without political stability these remain poorly exploited.

Lake Chad (right) is a large, shallow lake providing water and fish to more than 20 million people. It was one of the largest lakes in the world in 1823, but it has shrunk considerably since then, due to climate change and increased water use. In the 1960s it was the fourth-largest lake in Africa but is now under threat and could soon disappear altogether.

Q&A

Q: Is Equatorial Guinea on the equator?

A: Equatorial Guinea is very close to the equator, just one-degree north. The other country with a name like equator is Ecuador in Central America. There, the equator is just north of Ecuador's capital city of Quito.

Q: What is Nshima?

A: It is a food eaten in many parts of Africa, cooked from plain maize or corn meal (right). It's known as mealie-meal by the Zambians!

CAMEROON
Douala
Yaoundé
Malobo
EQUATORIAL GUINEA
Bangui
CENTRAL AFRICA REPUBLI
Congo
Libreville
Ogoué
Port Gentil
CONGO
Mbandaka
GABON
Lake Chad
Congo
DEMO
REP
Brazzaville
Pointe Noire
Kinshasa
OF
CABINDA (ANGOLA)
Matadi
Ka
Luanda
ANGOLA
Lobito
Huambo
Namibe
Cubango

0	150	300	450	600 miles
0	200	400	600	800	1000 kilometres

Fascinating Facts

Soccer is the most popular team game played in Cameroon, and the national team has done well in many World Cup tournaments.

Cocoa is grown in African plantations, but it originated in South America, brought over by the Belgians who wanted a reliable supply for their chocolate industry.

The rainforests of Gabon are home to the gorilla (below). Adult male gorillas eat about 70 lb (32 kg) of food per day. Adult females eat about two-thirds of that amount.

The people of Central Africa traditionally live in villages alongside others of their own tribe. Local materials are used for everything; homes are built of mud and thatch, and as electricity is rare, cooking is done over an open fire. Villagers try to grow their own food and keep animals, but when droughts or other disasters occur they can starve. With little medical help, the death rate is high.

Mount Ngaliema
(Mount Stanley)
16,765 ft
5,110 m

Kisangani

RWANDA

Kigali

Bujumbura

BURUNDI

Lake Tanganyika

Lake Mweru

Likasi

Kitwe

ZAMBIA

Lusaka

DATA BANK

Longest river
Congo 2,722 miles (4380km)

Highest mountain
Mont Ngaliema (Mount Stanley)
(Democratic Republic of Congo)
16,765 ft (5,110 m)

Coastline
2,083 miles (3,352 km)

Climate
Dry in northern Chad. Heavy rain all year along the equator. Very hot all year around.

Largest city and population
Kinshasa (Democratic Republic of Congo) 6,301,100

Annual income
US $1,000 or £550 approx. per person

East Africa

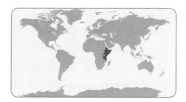

The geography of East Africa is often stunning and scenic. It is the site of Kilimanjaro and Mount Kenya, the two tallest peaks in Africa. The Great Rift Valley is a vast geographical and geological feature that runs north to south for some 3,000 miles (5,000 km), from northern Syria to central Mozambique. The unique geography and apparent suitability for farming made East Africa a target for European exploration in the 19th century.

Kenya, Tanzania and Uganda, are amongst the richer nations of sub-Saharan Africa. (Sub-Saharan Africa is the term used to describe those countries of the African continent that are not considered part of North Africa.) For many years they enjoyed a strong agricultural economy, with large tea and coffee plantations run by European colonialists. Ethiopia and Somalia to the north are poorer, having harsher climates and a history of civil wars. Kenya is the richest nation and attracts many tourists who go on safari to marvel at the many animals in the game reserves (above right). Much of the land is a high plateau with higher mountains. This keeps the inland climate from being too hot, and allows agriculture to prosper. The Great Rift Valley runs through the west of the region, and has many large lakes, such as Lake Nyasa and Lake Tanganyika.

Kenya is the world's third-largest producer of tea, after India and Sri Lanka. The climate in the hills is perfect for growing tea, with rain falling almost every afternoon. International companies, such as Brooke Bond, started the plantations.

DATA BANK

Longest river
Zambezi (Zambia, Angola, Botswana, Zimbabwe, Mozambique) 2,200 miles (3,540 km)

Highest mountain
Kilimanjaro (Tanzania) 19,341 ft (5,895 m)

Coastline
5,211 miles (8,386 km)

Climate
Wettest in the Uganda highlands and driest in Somalia. Hot but temperate in the highlands.

Largest city and population
Addis Ababa (Ethiopia) 2,638,500

Annual income
US $900 or £500 approx. per person

Ethiopia is the birthplace of coffee. More than 1,000 years ago, a goat herder in Ethiopia's highlands plucked a few red berries from the Kafa tree (right) and tasted them. He liked the flavour, and the pleasant effect that followed. Today the same berries, dried, roasted and ground, have become the world's second most popular non-alcoholic beverage after tea. Coffee accounts for 63% of Ethiopia's exports and about 25% of the population depend on coffee for their livelihood.

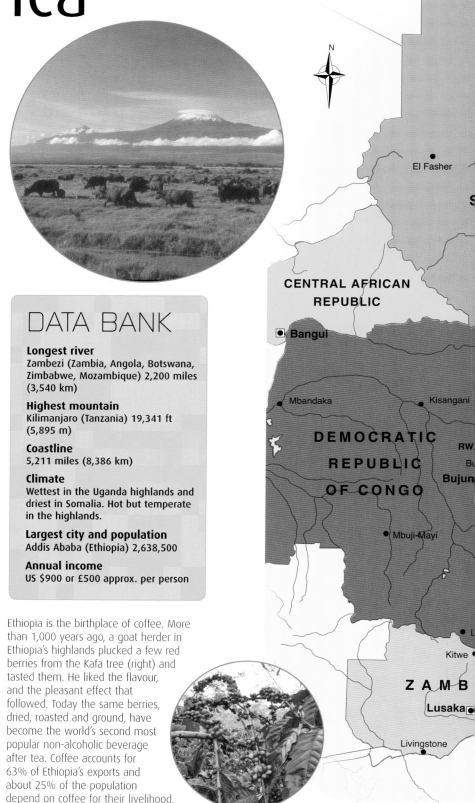

Wadi-Halfa

Port Sudan

Atbara

oum

Kassala

Asmera

ERITREA

Wad Medani

N

DJIBOUTI

Djibouti

Berbera

Addis Ababa

S O M A L I A

Dire Dawa

E T H I O P I A

Blue Nile

White Nile

UGANDA

K E N Y A

Mogadishu

npala

Kisumu

Tana

Kigali

Nairobi

Kismayu

Mwanza

Mount Kilimanjaro
19,341 ft
5,895 m

T A N Z A N I A

Mombasa

Dodoma

Zanzibar

Rufiji

Dar-es-Salaam

ALDABRA IS.

FARQUHAR IS.

MALAWAI

COMOROS

Lilongwe

Blantyre

```
0    150    300    450    600 miles
|----|------|------|------|
0   200  400  600  800  1000 kilometres
```

Fascinating Facts

Tororo, Uganda, has a world record average of 251 days of thunder each year.

The world's fastest mammal on land is the cheetah (below), which has a maximum speed of approximately 100 mph (161 km/h).

The tallest mammal is the giraffe (left), which grow to a height of around 18 ft (5.5 m).

Ethiopian and Kenyan athletes have an excellent record of track and marathon running in the Olympics and international competitions, in part due to the high altitudes at which they live.

Q&A

Q: What is the largest bird in the world?

A: The African ostrich (above), which reaches 9 ft (2.75 m) tall and weighs more than 330 lb (150 kg). Despite its size, the ostrich is also the fastest bird on land, reaching 45 mph (72 km/h), but cannot fly!

Q: How big is an elephant?

A: The male African bush elephant (above left) is the world's largest land mammal, being up to 13 ft (4m) tall at its shoulder and weighing about 12 tons.

Southern Africa

Southern Africa consists of Angola, Botswana, Lesotho, Madagascar, Malawi, Mozambique, Namibia, South Africa, Swaziland, Zambia and Zimbabwe. The geography of the land is varied, ranging from forest, grassland, desert, low-lying coastal areas, and mountains. The regions natural resources are diamonds, gold and uranium, and its wildlife species include the lion, leopard, elephant, and white rhino.

Madagascar is an island nation in the Indian Ocean, which lies off the eastern shore of the mainland. It has a wealth of animal and plant life, 80% of which are unique to the island. Madagascar's population is predominantly of mixed Asian and African origin. Recent research suggests that the island was uninhabited until about 1,500 years ago. The local people speak a language called Malagasy, and French is also spoken as the island was once a French colony.

Q&A

Q: How high are the Victoria Falls?

A: The Victoria Falls (right), also called Mosi-oa-Tunya, are 420 ft (128 m) high and are about 1 mile (1.7 km) wide. The Falls are situated on the border of Zambia and Zimbabwe.

Q: Why is the lemur only found on the island of Madagascar?

A: Madagascar's long isolation from neighbouring continents has resulted in a unique mix of plants and animals, many found nowhere else in the world.

ANGOLA

Benguela
Huambo
Lubango

Solwezi
Kitwe

ZAMBI

Lusaka

Mongu

Victoria Falls

ZIMBA

Bulawayo

NAMIBIA

Francistown

Windhoek

BOTSWANA

Walvis Bay

Gaborone

Pretoria
Johannesburg • Mbaba
SWA

Lüderitz

Orange

Thabana Ntle
11,424 ft
3,482 m

Bloemfontein • Maseru

LESOTHO

SOUTH AFRICA

Cape Town

East London
Port Elizabeth

| 0 | 150 | 300 | 450 | 600 miles |
| 0 | 200 | 400 | 600 | 800 | 1000 kilometres |

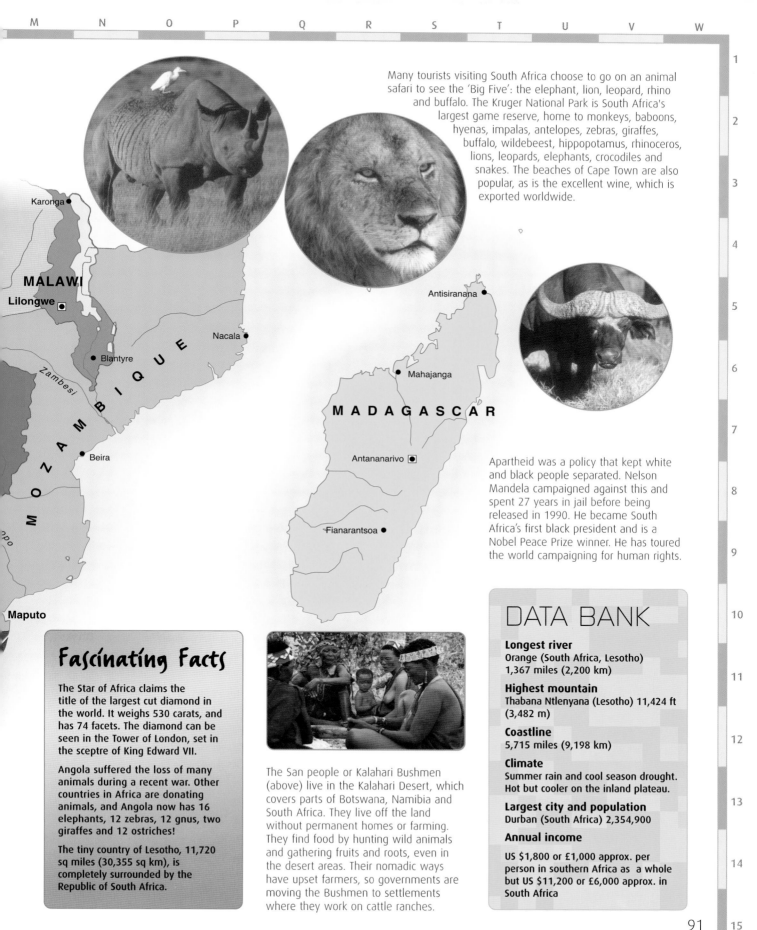

Many tourists visiting South Africa choose to go on an animal safari to see the 'Big Five': the elephant, lion, leopard, rhino and buffalo. The Kruger National Park is South Africa's largest game reserve, home to monkeys, baboons, hyenas, impalas, antelopes, zebras, giraffes, buffalo, wildebeest, hippopotamus, rhinoceros, lions, leopards, elephants, crocodiles and snakes. The beaches of Cape Town are also popular, as is the excellent wine, which is exported worldwide.

Karonga

MALAWI
Lilongwe ◙

MOZAMBIQUE
Zambesi

Blantyre
Nacala

Beira

Maputo

Antisiranana

Mahajanga

MADAGASCAR

Antananarivo ◙

Fianarantsoa

Apartheid was a policy that kept white and black people separated. Nelson Mandela campaigned against this and spent 27 years in jail before being released in 1990. He became South Africa's first black president and is a Nobel Peace Prize winner. He has toured the world campaigning for human rights.

Fascinating Facts

The Star of Africa claims the title of the largest cut diamond in the world. It weighs 530 carats, and has 74 facets. The diamond can be seen in the Tower of London, set in the sceptre of King Edward VII.

Angola suffered the loss of many animals during a recent war. Other countries in Africa are donating animals, and Angola now has 16 elephants, 12 zebras, 12 gnus, two giraffes and 12 ostriches!

The tiny country of Lesotho, 11,720 sq miles (30,355 sq km), is completely surrounded by the Republic of South Africa.

The San people or Kalahari Bushmen (above) live in the Kalahari Desert, which covers parts of Botswana, Namibia and South Africa. They live off the land without permanent homes or farming. They find food by hunting wild animals and gathering fruits and roots, even in the desert areas. Their nomadic ways have upset farmers, so governments are moving the Bushmen to settlements where they work on cattle ranches.

DATA BANK

Longest river
Orange (South Africa, Lesotho) 1,367 miles (2,200 km)

Highest mountain
Thabana Ntlenyana (Lesotho) 11,424 ft (3,482 m)

Coastline
5,715 miles (9,198 km)

Climate
Summer rain and cool season drought. Hot but cooler on the inland plateau.

Largest city and population
Durban (South Africa) 2,354,900

Annual income
US $1,800 or £1,000 approx. per person in southern Africa as a whole but US $11,200 or £6,000 approx. in South Africa

91

Asia

Stretching from the frozen Arctic Ocean to the Equatorial islands of Indonesia, Asia is the world's largest continent and contains the world's highest mountain, largest lake and lowest point.

Asia is rich in natural resources, such as petroleum, and forestry. Forestry is extensive throughout northern and eastern Asia, although many forest are being cut down to make way for agricultural products, such as rice and wheat (right).

Manufacturing has traditionally been strongest in East and Southeast Asia, particularly in China, Japan, Singapore and South Korea. The industry varies from manufacturing toys to high-tech products such as computers or cars – Japan has a thriving car industry. Many of the countries in the area are involved in the textile industry, and we see these clothes and shoes in Europe and the USA.

Q&A

Q: Are all of the islands of Indonesia Inhabited?

A: No. Approximately 7,000 of the islands are inhabited. They cover such an expanse of water that they spread over three time zones.

Q: Why do some women in Asia wear brass rings around their necks?

A: These women are from the Padaung – part of the Karen tribe of Thailand and Myanmar (right). There are many reasons given; some say it prevents them being bitten by tigers; others suggest it makes the women unattractive so they are less likely to be captured by slave traders. But some believe that a long neck is very attractive.

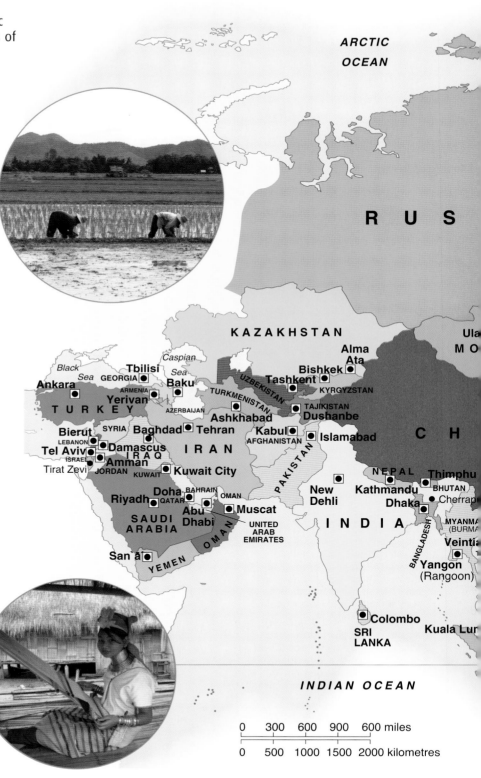

ARCTIC OCEAN

R U S

KAZAKHSTAN

Alma Ata

Bishkek

Tashkent

UZBEKISTAN

KYRGYZSTAN

Caspian Sea

Tbilisi

Baku

GEORGIA

TURKMENISTAN

TAJIKISTAN

Dushanbe

Ashkhabad

Black Sea

Ankara

ARMENIA

Yerivan

AZERBAIJAN

T U R K E Y

SYRIA

Baghdad

Tehran

Kabul

Islamabad

C H

AFGHANISTAN

Bierut

LEBANON

Damascus

I R A Q

I R A N

Tel Aviv

ISRAEL

Amman

PAKISTAN

NEPAL

Thimphu

Tirat Zevi

JORDAN

KUWAIT

Kuwait City

New Dehli

Kathmandu

BHUTAN

Dhaka

Cherrap

Doha

BAHRAIN

OMAN

I N D I A

Riyadh

QATAR

MYANMA (BURMA)

SAUDI ARABIA

Abu Dhabi

Muscat

UNITED ARAB EMIRATES

BANGLADESH

Veintia

O M A N

San á

YEMEN

Yangon (Rangoon)

Colombo

SRI LANKA

Kuala Lur

Ula MO

INDIAN OCEAN

0	300	600	900	600 miles

0	500	1000	1500	2000 kilometres

N

A

Verkhoyansk

DATA BANK

Longest river
Chang Jiang (Yangtze) (China) 3,964 miles (6,380 km)

Highest mountain
Everest (Nepal/Tibet) 29,035 ft (8,850 m)

Climate
Central and southwest Asia ranges from steppe to desert, with large areas having little or no rain. Snow on high ground. Heavy rain in east during summer monsoon.

Natural Resources
Oil, gas, coal and minerals

Population
1,306,313,812

Richest / poorest country
Japan is the richest country in Asia. East Timor is the poorest country.

The Philippines is a cluster of 7,107 islands with a total land area of approximately 116,000 sq miles (300,000 sq km). An archipelago is a group or cluster of islands. The islands are commonly divided into three island groups: Luzon, Visayas and Mindanao. The busy port of Manila, on Luzon, is the national capital. However Indonesia has over 17,000 islands!

Over 600 languages are spoken in Indonesia, whilst Korea, on the other hand, is home to only one language.

Vladivostock

A

Beijing

Pyongyang NORTH KOREA

A

Seoul SOUTH KOREA

JAPAN

Tokyo

Taiwan

Hong Kong

NAM

Manilla

PHILIPPINES

om Penn

dar Seri awan

BRUNEI

YSIA

pore

INDONESIA

Fascinating Facts

A collection of over 8,000 life-size terracotta warriors (above left) and horses was discovered in 1974 in the Shaanzi province in China. They had been buried with the first Emperor of Qin, Shi Huang around 210–209 BC. Today they are known as the Terracotta Army. 700,000 workmen took 38 years to complete the work.

Mount Everest (left) has grown by 6.5 ft (2 m) in the last 80 years due to geological movement

About Asia

The countries of Asia, their capital cities and population:

Afghanistan	Kabul	29,928,987
Armenia	Yerevan	2,982,904
Azerbaijan	Baku	7,911,974
Bahrain	Manama	688,345
Bangladesh	Dhaka	144,319,628
Bhutan	Thimphu	2,232,291
Brunei /Darussalam	Bandar Seri Begawan	372,361
Burma (Myanmar)	Rangoon	42,909,464
Cambodia	Phnom Penh	13,607,069
China	Beijing	1,306,313,812
East Timor	Dili	1,040,880
India	New Delhi	1,027,015,247
Indonesia	Jakarta	54,716,547
Iran	Teheran	68,017,860
Iraq	Baghdad	26,074,906
Israel	Jerusalem	6,276,883
Japan	Tokyo	127,417,244
Jordan	Amman	5,759,732
Kazakhstan	Astana	15,185,844
Korea (North)	Pyongyang	22,912,177
Korea (South)	Seoul	48,422,644
Kuwait	Kuwait City	2,335,648
Kyrgyzstan	Bishkek	5,146,281
Laos	Vientiane	6,217,141
Lebanon	Beirut	3,826,018
Malaysia	Kuala Lumpur	25,675, 677
Maldives	Male	349,106
Mongolia	Ulan Bator	2,791,272
Nepal	Kathmandu	27,676,547
Oman	Muscat	2,713,462
Pakistan	Islamabad	162,419,946
Philippines	Manila	87,857,473
Qatar	Doha	863,051
Russia	Moscow	6,692,865
Saudi Arabia	Riyadh	26,417,599
Singapore	Singapore	4,425,720
Sri Lanka	Colombo	19,340,512
Syria	Damascus	18,448,752
Tajikistan	Dushanbe	7,163,506
Thailand	Bangkok	64,865,523
Turkey	Ankara	69,660,559
Turkmenistan	Ashgabat	4,952,081
United Arab Emirates	Abu Dhabi	2,563,212
Uzbekistan	Tashkent	26,851,195
Vietnam	Hanoi	83,535,576
Yemen	Sana	20,727,063

Famous people

- Mahatma Ghandi (1869–1948). Led India peacefully to independence in 1947, before being assassinated by a Hindu rebel (right).

- Vladimir Lenin (1870 –1924). Led the successful Russian revolution which overthrew the Tsarist regime and established the first Communist state, called the Union of Soviet Socialist Republics – USSR.

- Aung San Suu Kyi (born 1945). Was awarded the Nobel Peace Prize in 1991 for her part in trying to establish democracy in Myanmar.

- Confucius (551–479 BC). The sayings of Confucius still have a great influence on the Chinese people.

- Peter Tchaikovsky (1840–93). Russia's most well-known classical composer, especially famous for his ballets 'Swan Lake' and 'The Nutcracker' (right).

Land use

- Asia contains over 75% of the world's oil and gas reserves. Arabia has 10% of the world's needs.

- Russia has plentiful supplies of oil and gas but they are difficult to source as they are under Siberia's frozen landmass.

- The two most heavily populated countries in the world, China and India, are in Asia; they are also the two fastest growing economies.

- India and China and the huge area of the Russian Steppes are losing their communities as people leave the land to find work in the booming new industrial areas.

- There is an enormous contrast between the lives of the rich and those of the poor in this continent.

Languages

- All Arab countries speak Arabic, but in Iran, Farsi is spoken.

Industry

- During the 1930s Russia (then part of the Soviet Union) developed heavy industries and industrialised its farming methods. Initially, this enabled them to catch up with the much more developed West, but it came at great cost to the environment.

- Today, both India and China are developing their industries and the challenge for them, and the world as a whole, is how to do this without endangering the planet.

- After 1945 Japan grew to be one of the largest economies, producing most of the world's electronic products.

- Tourism. The Far Eastern countries of China, Vietnam, Cambodia and Thailand, which were once closed off to the western world, are now becoming among the most popular tourist destinations. People are drawn to a totally different culture and life-style, and the numerous fabulous ancient monuments and temples such as the Taj Mahal below.

Population

The rising population in this part of the world is causing concern. Asians make up 56% of the earth's population, although they occupy just over 31% of the planet's arable land.

- Many countries cannot afford to build enough schools or hospitals, or to provide enough jobs.

- Increasingly, large cities produce more and more pollution.

- Access to clean water is essential to health, yet millions are denied this. Access to water could be the cause of future conflicts, as growing populations compete for declining resources.

- Poorer peoples in countries where there is little support from the State, need larger families, as the older generations rely on the young ones for support in old age.

- Experts expect that populations in Asia (with the exception of Japan) will continue to grow, in particular in countries where there are already shortages of natural resources.

- China introduced a policy of 'one child per family' in order to control its population growth.

- More food is needed, but land suitable for farming is decreasing. Excessive deforestation causes soil erosion and over-grazing can turn grassland to desert.

Transport

- The longest railroad in the world is the Trans-Siberian Railway, which connects Moscow with Vladivostok on the Pacific coast. It is 5,744 miles (9,244 km) and the journey takes eight days.

- There are thought to be 300 million bicycles in China.

- Shinkansen are the high speed trains in Japan, and they are known as 'bullet trains'. The fastest shinkansen train is the 500 series 'Nozomi' which operates at a maximum speed of 186 mph (300 km/h).

Natural features

- In Bangladesh half the country was underwater following heavy monsoon rains in 2004. Up to 20 million people were marooned or made homeless. A government official said, 'They have no shelter, their crops are damaged and there are health hazards. If it continues for long we cannot save them'.

- The Maldives consists of a group of atolls in the Indian Ocean. An atoll is a type of low, coral island, found in the tropical oceans. There are 26 atolls, made up of almost 1,200 tiny islands (islets), 200 of which are inhabited by people.

- The Himalayan Mountains are the world's largest range, with eight peaks over 26,247 ft (8,000 m) – the highest is Everest at 29,035 ft (8,850 m). It stretches from Pakistan in the west to Myanmar in the East (below).

- Large parts of Asia are subject to severe earthquakes and other natural disasters. This is especially true of the countries bordering the Pacific from Indonesia to Japan, as shifting tectonic plates follow this coast.

Environment

- Much of Russia is severely polluted especially around the oil fields of the Caspian Sea.

- On August 6, 1945, a nuclear weapon was dropped on Hiroshima, Japan, killing an estimated 80,000 people and heavily damaging 80% of the city. In the following months, an estimated 60,000 more people died from injuries or radiation poisoning. Since 1945, several thousand have died of illnesses caused by the bomb. The Torii (gate) to the Shrine at Miyajima on Itsukushima Island is much photographed by visitors to Hiroshima. Itsukushima Island is considered to be sacred.

Turkey

The Republic of Turkey straddles the continents of both Europe and Asia by means of two 0.6 mile (1 km) long bridges over the narrow Bosporus Strait which links the Black Sea with the Mediterranean.

Turkey is mountainous, with a high central plateau and a narrow coastal plain. The most visited regions are Istanbul and the Mediterranean tourist resorts. Turkey borders Syria, Iraq and Iran, and also claims ownership of Northern Cyprus. Whilst mainly in Asia, Turkey hopes to become a member of the European Union in an effort to modernise its farms and increase its trade with the west.

The country is famous for Turkish Delight, which is a confection made from starch and sugar, often flavoured with rosewater or lemon. Popular at Christmas, it has a soft, sticky consistency, and is often packaged in small cubes that are dusted with sugar to prevent sticking.

Fascinating Facts

Mohair is produced from the wool of the Turkish Angora goat.

The first president of Turkey in 1923, was given the name Ataturk, which means 'father of the Turks'.

The 500-year-old Grand Bazaar in Istanbul (right) is one of the largest covered markets in the world, with more than 58 streets. Between 4,000 and 400,000 visitors come to see its jewellery, pottery, spice and carpet shops daily.

Edirne, Istanbul, Adapazari, **Ankara**, Bursa, Eskisehir, Eskisehir, Lake Tuz, Konya, Izmir, Aydin, Antalya, Alanya

0 120 240 miles
0 100 200 300 400 kilometres

DATA BANK

Longest river
Kizilirmak 715 miles (1,150 km)

Highest mountain
Mount Ararat (The Great Mount Agri)
16,854 (5,137 m)

Coastline
4,474 miles (7,200 km)

Climate
Very wet along the north coast but dry in interior. Cold, snowy winters inland, with hot, dry summers.

Largest city and population
Istanbul 9,216,400

Annual income
US $7,400 or £4,000 approx per person

With high unemployment, especially outside the industrial cities of Istanbul and Ankara, over a million Turks have sought employment abroad, especially in Germany. They send money home.

Turkish restaurants are found worldwide. Classic Turkish cuisine offers cubes of grilled meat on a skewer (a kebab), rice, pitta bread and houmous, together with tomatoes, garlic, olives and olive oil. A 'meze' consisting of a number of small dishes may be served before the main course of a meal.

Q&A

Q: What is a Trojan horse?

A: The Trojan army could not defeat the city of Troy (an ancient city situated in present-day Turkey) 3,000 years ago, so they tricked their way in with a wooden horse full of soldiers. These soldiers opened the city gates after the horse was pulled into Troy. The ruins of Troy are now a tourist site (left).

Q: Did Noah's Ark come to rest in Turkey?

A: After the Biblical flood, the ark is said to have landed on Mount Ararat, although no remains have been found. It is a dormant volcanic peak in the far northeast corner of Turkey.

Ankara, which replaced Istanbul as the capital of Turkey in 1923, is the centre of the Turkish Government. It is home to all foreign embassies, is strategically located at the centre of Turkey's highway and rail network and serves as the marketing centre for the surrounding agricultural area.

Map labels: Hopa, Trabzon, amsun, Tokat, Sivas, Elâzig, Diyarbakir, Mardin, Gaziantep, aniye, dana, Iskenderun, seri, KEY, Erzerum, Mount Ararat 16,854 ft 5,137 m, Lake Van, 40°, 45°, 35°

97

The Near East

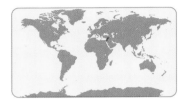

The Near East is a region of just four countries: Israel, Jordan, Lebanon and Syria. This is a desert area with very little natural water. Israel, Lebanon and Syria have a Mediterranean coastline, but only Israel has the financial ability to set up effective irrigation systems.

Apart from the coastal strip, Syria, Lebanon, and Jordan are largely desert. Israel is a much more wealthy country and has developed world-class, high-value industries such as computer software development (partly due to help from the USA). This has also been helped by the highly-educated workforce and by the immigration of skilled Jews in the 1990s from Russia.

Jordan consists mostly of dry desert in the east, with a Highland area to the west. The Great Rift Valley of the River Jordan separates Jordan and Israel. The highest point in the country is Jabal Ram at 5,689 ft (1,734 m). The country's capital is Amman in the northwest.

DATA BANK

Longest river
Jordan River (Lebanon, Syria)
223 miles (359 km)

Highest mountain
Qurnat as Sawda' (Lebanon) 10,131 ft
(3,088 m)

Coastline
446 miles (717 km)

Climate
Winter rain on the coast and mountains. Very dry summers. Very hot summers. Mild winters with snow in the mountains

Largest city and population
Aleppo (Halab) (Syria) 1,891,900

Annual income
US $20,800 or £12,000 approx. per person in Israel, US $4,400 or £2,500 approx. elsewhere

The River Euphrates flows through the Syrian Desert, and in 1973 The Tabaqah Dam was completed to create Lake Assad (above). The lake provides 20% of Syria's electricity and has doubled Syria's irrigated land. However the project has not been as successful as planned, due to other dams which reduce the water flow.

Trip

LEBANON

Beirut

Haifa

Irb

Nablus

Tel Aviv

West Bank

Jerusalem

Gaza Strip

Gaza

Dead

ISRAEL

J

Elat

Al 'Aqabah

Jordan

Tigris

Al Qamishli

• Halab

Euphrates

yah

• Hims

as Sawda'
ft
m

S Y R I A

amascus

a

O
A N

Fascinating Facts

Israel has the highest number of solar-powered water heaters in the world, these are installed in more than 80% of Israeli households.

The world's heaviest lemon was grown by Aharon Shemoel on his farm in Israel. It weighed 12 lb (5.3 kg) on January 8, 2003.

It is thought that Moses is buried on Mount Nebo.

The Arabic name for Lebanon is 'Lubnan' which means white – the colour of the Lebanese mountains covered in snow.

Traditionally, agriculture consists of the keeping of herds of sheep and goats (below). Where irrigation is possible, vegetables and fruit are grown, and much of it exported to Europe. Irrigation water comes from the Jordan River, which flows south through the Sea of Galilee into the Dead Sea.

Lebanon is a small country with an extraordinarily rich and vibrant culture. It has many ethnic groups who contribute to the country's food, musical and literary traditions, and festivals. The capital city, Beirut, in particular has a very active arts scene, with fashion shows, exhibitions, and concerts held throughout the year in its galleries, museums, theatres, and public spaces. Lebanese society is modern, educated, and comparable to European societies of the Mediterranean.

Q&A

Q: What is the Wailing Wall (above left)?

A: When the Romans destroyed Solomon's temple 2,000 years ago, only the western wall remained. Only since 1976 have Jews been able to pray there. Many cry with emotion, hence the name Wailing Wall.

Q: Why is Israel's largest lake called the Dead Sea?

A: This lake (left) is so salty that its water cannot be used for irrigation as it kills plants. The Dead Sea is 1,312 ft (400 m) below sea level and the water flowing into it evaporates, making it very salty.

50   100 miles

100   200 kilometres

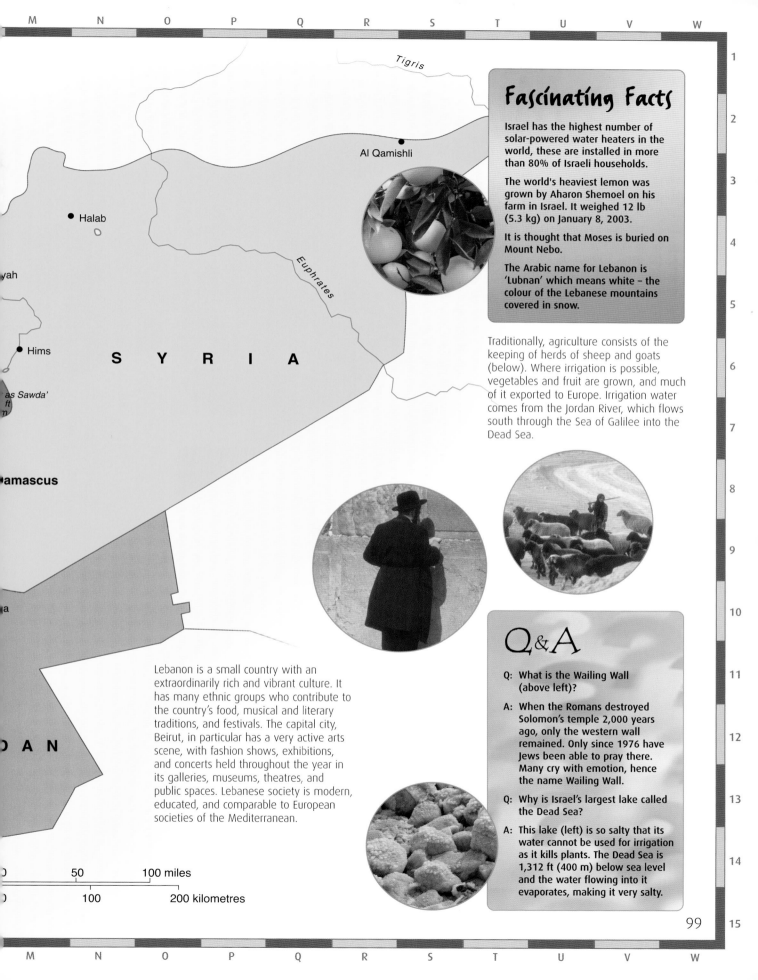

The Middle East

The area known as The Middle East includes the countries of Armenia, Azerbaijan, Bahrain, Iran, Iraq, Kuwait, Oman, Qatar, Saudi Arabia, United Arab Emirates and Yemen. The climate of this region is generally harsh, dry desert, often with temperatures that are either very high or very low. Although these countries are very rich in oil, they lack water – there are very few rivers apart from the Euphrates in Iraq.

Although the area is now almost all desert, 6,000 years ago this was the most advanced part of the world, with the great civilisation of Mesopotamia located between the River Euphrates and the River Tigris. Mesopotamia's ancient wealth was due to the hot, sunny climate combined with the fertile soil and irrigation water provided by the two rivers. Today the region's wealth comes from selling oil.

Yemen, without oil reserves, is much poorer. Only 3% of the land is suitable for farming. Here they grow grain, fruits, vegetables, pulses, coffee, and cotton, and keep livestock (sheep, goats, cattle and camels, bottom right).

Increased wealth and modern lifestyles have led to an increased demand for water. Massive desalination plants, fuelled by oil and gas, remove the salt from seawater. The United Arab Emirates provides over 80% of its water supply in this way.

The traditional way of life was dependent on the herding of goats, moving through the desert in search of pasture. The Bedouin tribes of the Arabian desert still live in tents (above and right) woven from goat hair, and, to supplement their diet, they collect roots, bird's eggs, jerboas, lizards, rabbits and locusts.

Fascinating Facts

Saudi Arabia is the world's largest producer of desalinated water. This means that the salt is taken out of the sea water so that people can drink it.

About one million foreign Muslim visitors a year attend Al Hajj (or The Pilgrimage) to Mecca (the capital city of Saudi Arabia).

When an Omani woman dies, her jewellery is melted down and sold.

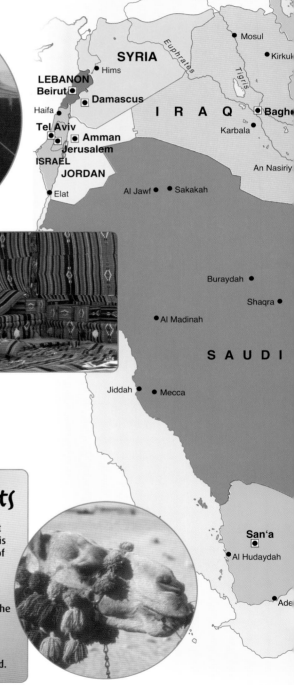

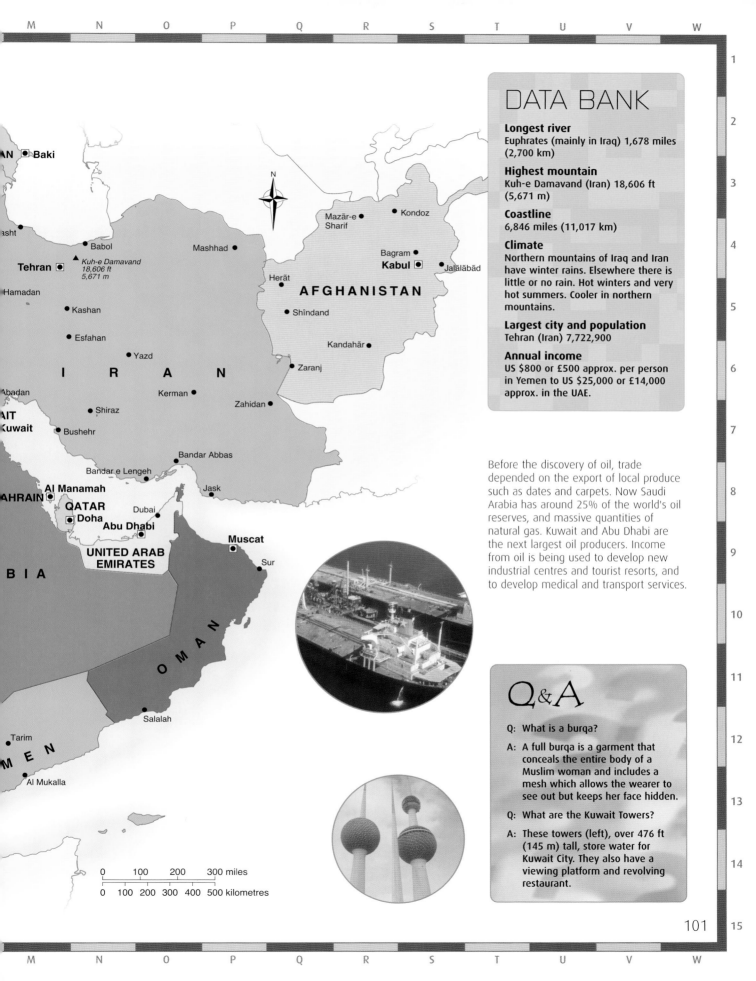

Baki

asht

Babol

Mashhad

Tehran ▣ ▲ Kuh-e Damavand
18,606 ft
5,671 m

Hamadan

Kashan

Esfahan

I R A N

Yazd

Abadan

Shiraz

Kerman

AIT
Kuwait

Bushehr

Zahidan

Bandar Abbas

Bandar e Lengeh

Jask

Al Manamah

AHRAIN ▣

QATAR
▣ Doha

Abu Dhabi
▣

Dubai

UNITED ARAB
EMIRATES

BIA

O M A N

MEN

M E N

Tarim

Al Mukalla

Salalah

Muscat
▣

Sur

N

Mazār-e
Sharif

Kondoz

Bagram

Kabul ▣ Jalālābād

Herāt

AFGHANISTAN

Shîndand

Kandahār

Zaranj

DATA BANK

Longest river
Euphrates (mainly in Iraq) 1,678 miles
(2,700 km)

Highest mountain
Kuh-e Damavand (Iran) 18,606 ft
(5,671 m)

Coastline
6,846 miles (11,017 km)

Climate
Northern mountains of Iraq and Iran
have winter rains. Elsewhere there is
little or no rain. Hot winters and very
hot summers. Cooler in northern
mountains.

Largest city and population
Tehran (Iran) 7,722,900

Annual income
US $800 or £500 approx. per person
in Yemen to US $25,000 or £14,000
approx. in the UAE.

Before the discovery of oil, trade
depended on the export of local produce
such as dates and carpets. Now Saudi
Arabia has around 25% of the world's oil
reserves, and massive quantities of
natural gas. Kuwait and Abu Dhabi are
the next largest oil producers. Income
from oil is being used to develop new
industrial centres and tourist resorts, and
to develop medical and transport services.

Q&A

Q: What is a burqa?

A: A full burqa is a garment that
conceals the entire body of a
Muslim woman and includes a
mesh which allows the wearer to
see out but keeps her face hidden.

Q: What are the Kuwait Towers?

A: These towers (left), over 476 ft
(145 m) tall, store water for
Kuwait City. They also have a
viewing platform and revolving
restaurant.

0   100   200   300 miles

0 100 200 300 400 500 kilometres

Russia east of the Urals

All of Russia that is east of the Ural Mountain range is also called the Russian Federation. This part of Russia is the largest country on earth, spanning over 6,500,000 sq miles (17,000,000 sq km). Bordered by the Arctic Ocean to the north, the climate is harsh, and even on the southern borders with China and Outer Mongolia farming is limited to keeping a few animals. Despite the fact that the area has large amounts of oil, gas, uranium, coal and timber, living standards are low, hampered by the vast distances to markets in the west, the frozen ground, and years of Communist rule. Kazakhstan, on its southern border, is a huge country which covers a territory equivalent to the whole of Western Europe and has vast mineral resources and enormous economic potential.

DATA BANK

Longest river
Ob 3,459 miles (5,534 km)

Highest mountain
Pik Pobeda (or Tömür Teng), Kyrgyzstan, 24,407 ft (7,439 m)

Coastline
19,497 miles (31,377 km)

Climate
From subarctic in Siberia, to tundra climate in the polar north. Winters vary from cool to frigid; summers vary from warm in the steppes to cool along Arctic coast.

Largest city and population
Novosibirsk (Russia) 1,396,800

Annual income
US $11,100 or £6,500 approx. per person

The Aral Sea, straddling the Uzbekistan and Kazakhstan border, has decreased 80% in volume since 1960. Much of the water flowing into the lake was diverted by the Soviet government to irrigate farmland. Not only did the lake shrink, but the remaining water became very salty, killing off many fish, so that by 1979 the commercial fishing industry closed.

The nomadic Mongolian people live in sturdy portable *gers*.

Q&A

Q: Which is the longest railway in the world?

A: The Trans-Siberian railway is 5,571 miles (9,288 km) long and runs between Moscow and Vladivostok on the Pacific coast. It was constructed between 1891 and 1916 to protect Russian Pacific Ocean territories. It remains the main overland route across Russia.

Q. Does Siberia really have salt mines?

A: It did, but only in the very west of the area, in the Ural Mountains. Salt isn't mined there any more, however, one old mine is now a museum.

120°   160°   80°

ARCTIC OCEAN

East Siberian Sea

Lena

NTRAL BERIAN ATEAU

B E R I A

Kolyma Lowland

Indigirka

Kolyma

Yakutsk

Lena

Aldan

Magadan

Sea of Okhotsk

I A

Lake Baykal

Trans-Siberian Railway

Khabarovsk

Vladivostok

A

Sea of Japan

PACIFIC OCEAN

40°

160°

120°

| 0 | 600 | 1200 | 1800 | 2400 miles |
| 0 | 1000 | 2000 | 3000 | 4000 kilometres |

The mountains bordering Mongolia are home to the rare Siberian Ibex (left), whose front legs are shorter that its back ones, enabling it to climb mountains easily. Its hooves give it exceptional balance. The male has horns which can be 5 ft (1.5m) long.

Fascinating Facts

The greatest temperature range recorded is in Verkhoyansk, Siberia dropping to −90° F (−68 °C) yet rising to 99° F (37 °C).

The world's deepest lake is Lake Baikal, in Siberia, Russia with a depth of 5,371 ft (1,637 m), of which 3,875 ft (1,181m) are below sea level. It is also the oldest freshwater lake on Earth, and contains one-fifth of all the world's fresh surface water!

The vast, sparsely-populated coniferous forests of northern Russia, known as the Taiga, cover 40% of the region. The underlying soil is permanently frozen so the trees are small, and in the summer the top layer melts to create marshy land unsuited to farming.

The Russian Cyrillic alphabet was devised by Greek missionaries 1,000 years ago. It is closely based on the Greek alphabet, with about a dozen additional letters invented to represent Slavic sounds not found in Greek. Changes were made up to 1918, leaving the alphabet (right) as it is today.

ТЕХНИЧЕСКАЯ ИНСПЕКЦИЯ ТРУДА по Московской области

103

India and south Asia

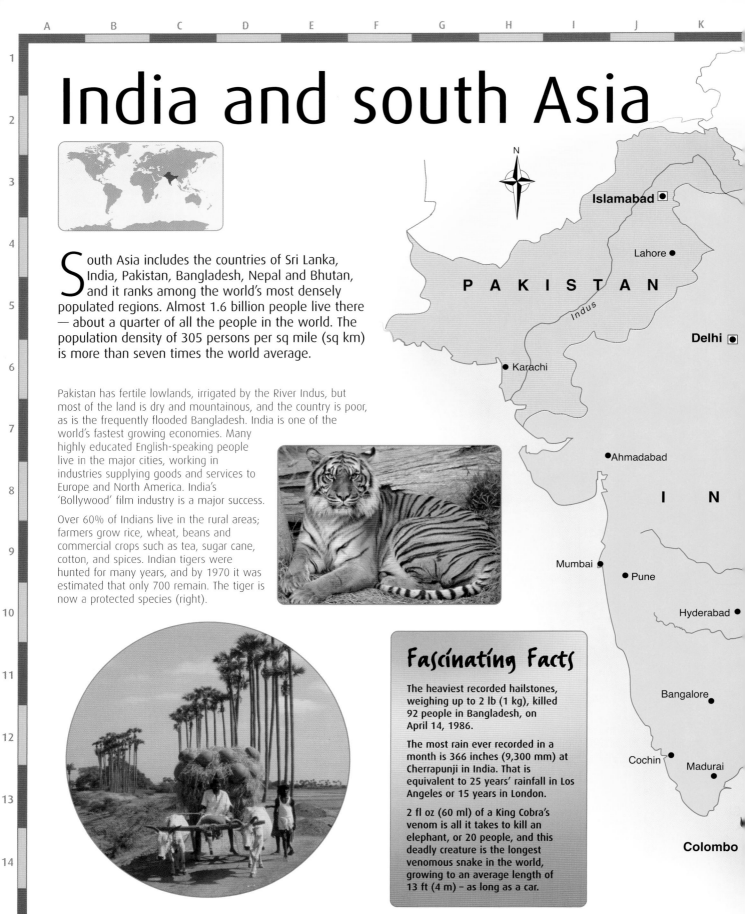

S outh Asia includes the countries of Sri Lanka, India, Pakistan, Bangladesh, Nepal and Bhutan, and it ranks among the world's most densely populated regions. Almost 1.6 billion people live there — about a quarter of all the people in the world. The population density of 305 persons per sq mile (sq km) is more than seven times the world average.

Pakistan has fertile lowlands, irrigated by the River Indus, but most of the land is dry and mountainous, and the country is poor, as is the frequently flooded Bangladesh. India is one of the world's fastest growing economies. Many highly educated English-speaking people live in the major cities, working in industries supplying goods and services to Europe and North America. India's 'Bollywood' film industry is a major success.

Over 60% of Indians live in the rural areas; farmers grow rice, wheat, beans and commercial crops such as tea, sugar cane, cotton, and spices. Indian tigers were hunted for many years, and by 1970 it was estimated that only 700 remain. The tiger is now a protected species (right).

Islamabad ◻

PAKISTAN

Lahore ●

Indus

Delhi ◻

● Karachi

● Ahmadabad

I N

Mumbai ● ● Pune

Hyderabad ●

Bangalore ●

Cochin ● ● Madurai

Colombo

Fascinating Facts

The heaviest recorded hailstones, weighing up to 2 lb (1 kg), killed 92 people in Bangladesh, on April 14, 1986.

The most rain ever recorded in a month is 366 inches (9,300 mm) at Cherrapunji in India. That is equivalent to 25 years' rainfall in Los Angeles or 15 years in London.

2 fl oz (60 ml) of a King Cobra's venom is all it takes to kill an elephant, or 20 people, and this deadly creature is the longest venomous snake in the world, growing to an average length of 13 ft (4 m) - as long as a car.

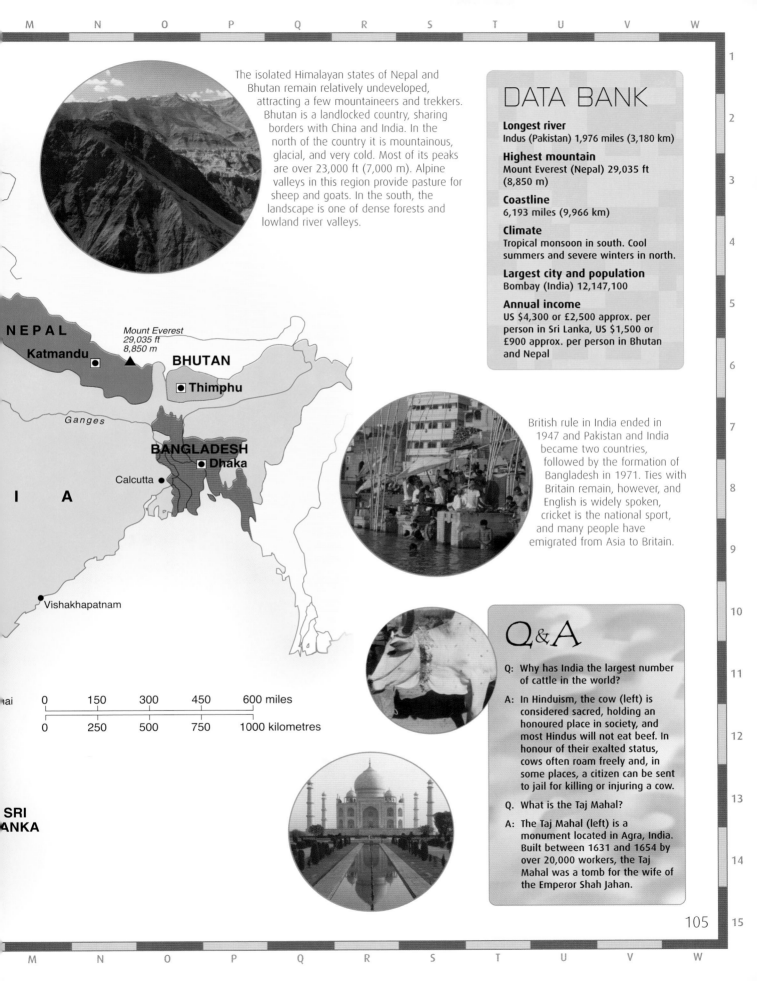

The isolated Himalayan states of Nepal and Bhutan remain relatively undeveloped, attracting a few mountaineers and trekkers. Bhutan is a landlocked country, sharing borders with China and India. In the north of the country it is mountainous, glacial, and very cold. Most of its peaks are over 23,000 ft (7,000 m). Alpine valleys in this region provide pasture for sheep and goats. In the south, the landscape is one of dense forests and lowland river valleys.

DATA BANK

Longest river
Indus (Pakistan) 1,976 miles (3,180 km)

Highest mountain
Mount Everest (Nepal) 29,035 ft (8,850 m)

Coastline
6,193 miles (9,966 km)

Climate
Tropical monsoon in south. Cool summers and severe winters in north.

Largest city and population
Bombay (India) 12,147,100

Annual income
US $4,300 or £2,500 approx. per person in Sri Lanka, US $1,500 or £900 approx. per person in Bhutan and Nepal

NEPAL
Katmandu
Mount Everest 29,035 ft 8,850 m
BHUTAN
Thimphu
Ganges
BANGLADESH
Dhaka
Calcutta
I A
Vishakhapatnam

| 0 | 150 | 300 | 450 | 600 miles |
| 0 | 250 | 500 | 750 | 1000 kilometres |

SRI ANKA

British rule in India ended in 1947 and Pakistan and India became two countries, followed by the formation of Bangladesh in 1971. Ties with Britain remain, however, and English is widely spoken, cricket is the national sport, and many people have emigrated from Asia to Britain.

Q&A

Q: Why has India the largest number of cattle in the world?

A: In Hinduism, the cow (left) is considered sacred, holding an honoured place in society, and most Hindus will not eat beef. In honour of their exalted status, cows often roam freely and, in some places, a citizen can be sent to jail for killing or injuring a cow.

Q. What is the Taj Mahal?

A: The Taj Mahal (left) is a monument located in Agra, India. Built between 1631 and 1654 by over 20,000 workers, the Taj Mahal was a tomb for the wife of the Emperor Shah Jahan.

Southeast Asia

The tropical region south of China comprises Vietnam, Laos, Cambodia, Thailand and Myanmar (Burma). To the south lie Malaysia, Singapore and Indonesia. Most people live near the coast, away from the thickly forested mountainous interior, and are still mainly dependent on fishing and farming. Rice is the main crop, grown in river valleys in wet paddy fields.

Thailand is developing both electronics manufacturing and tourist industries. Wars in Vietnam and Cambodia devastated many cities, and Cambodia has the highest number of widows and orphans in the world. Indonesia consists of over 13,000 islands, including Bali, Java, and Sumatra. Malaysia is developing rapidly, with car and shipbuilding industries. Singapore is the richest country in the region, with high educational standards, and is one of the world's major ports and trading centres.

Q&A

Q: What is the longest snake in the world?

A: The reticulated python of Southeast Asia regularly exceeds 20 ft (6 m). The longest ever was 33 ft (10 m), in Indonesia.

Q: Are elephants still used by man?

A: Yes, especially in the forests of Burma and Thailand, where they are used to move logs.

Hkakabo Razi
19,295 ft
5,881 m

MYANMAR

LAOS

Hanoi

Vientiane

Mekong

Hue
Da Nang

Yangon

THAILAND

Moulmein

Bangkok

CAMBODIA

VIETNAM

Phnom Penh

Ho Chi Minh

Kota Kinabalu

Bander Seri Begawan
BRUNEI

MALAYSIA

SARAWAK

Medan

Kuala Lumpur

SINGAPORE

Kuching

Pontianak

KALIMANTAN

SUMATRA

IND

Jakarta

Semarang   JAVA

The warm sea and attractive coast of Thailand and Myanmar have attracted many tourists.

The tsunami that struck southeast Asia on December 26, 2004, has been confirmed as the most devastating in modern history. The series of waves was caused by an earthquake off the coast of northern Sumatra that measured 9.0 on the Richter scale and forced the seabed to rise by between 16 and 100 ft (5 and 30 m).

Fascinating Facts

Most young men in Thailand become Buddhist monks (left) for a short time, and shaven-headed monks ask for alms (gifts of food) from the local people. Each monk is given an alms bowl when he joins the religious community.

In Bangkok, goods can be bought from floating markets, where produce is sold from boats (left).

The water buffalo (below) is a work animal, and provides 20–30% of the power on farms in Thailand, Indonesia, Malaysia, the Philippines, and Burma. It is used to plough, level the land, haul carts, pump water, carry people, press sugar cane, haul logs, and much, much more.

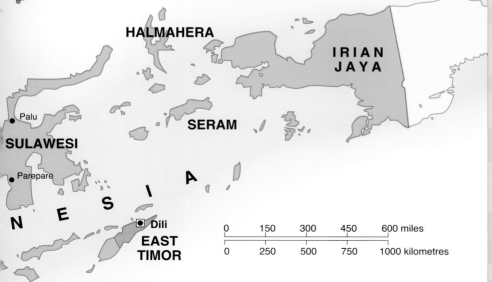

Rice and rice noodles are the staple food, eaten with vegetables, meat and fish. Food is often spicy, and hot peppers are popular. Fish sauce is used in many recipes. Fast food, Asian-style, is cooked in market stalls, and even on mobile, floating stalls (left) in the creeks of coastal cities.

PHILIPPINES

HALMAHERA

IRIAN JAYA

SERAM

Palu

SULAWESI

NESIA

Parepare

Dili

EAST TIMOR

| 0 | 150 | 300 | 450 | 600 miles |
| 0 | 250 | 500 | 750 | 1000 kilometres |

DATA BANK

Longest river
Mekong (China, Myanmar, Laos, Thailand, Cambodia, Vietnam) 3,293 miles (5,300 km)

Highest mountain
Hkakbo Razi (Myanmar) 19,295 ft (5,881 m)

Coastline
65,187 miles (104,909 km)

Climate
Tropical; annual monsoon in southwest (April to October) and in northeast (October to February).

Largest city and population
Bangkok (Thailand) 9,000,000

Annual income
US $1,700 or £1,000 approx per person in Burma, US $28,100 or £16,000 approx per person in Singapore

China

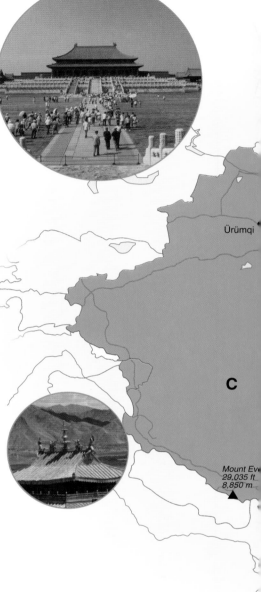

China, the world's most populous country, has a continuous culture stretching back nearly 4,000 years, and is now the world's fastest-growing economy. The current industrial growth is concentrated in manufacturing household goods and clothing, resulting in China being the largest oil consumer after the US, and the world's biggest producer and consumer of coal.

The rapid industrialisation has created vast differences between the wealth of urban workers and those remaining as peasant farmers. Pollution is a major issue, but in recent years the government has announced a wish to slow economic growth and to solve some of the problems it has caused.

Fascinating Facts

The highest earthquake death-toll in modern times was caused by one hitting Tangshan, China, on July 28, 1976, with an official figure of 655,237 deaths.

At 2,150 miles (3,460 km) long, the Great Wall of China is the longest wall in the world (right), nearly three times the length of Britain. It also has 2,193 miles (3,530 km) of branches and spurs. It is said to be the only human-made structure that is visible to the naked eye from the moon.

Over 600 years ago China led the world in technology, inventing paper, printing, gunpowder, the magnetic compass and porcelain.

There has been a massive investment in hydroelectric power, including the Three Gorges Dam project, which is to dam the Yangtze River. The dam is 607 ft (185 m) high, and 7,575 ft (2,309 m) long. Once running at full capacity, it will have a capacity of more than 18,000 megawatts, making it the world's largest hydroelectric generating station. China also hopes that the dam will help control flooding on the Yangtze River, which in the past has claimed hundreds of thousands of lives.

On some of the rivers of China, fishermen catch fish without nets or hooks by using cormorants. The birds have a ring put round their neck to stop them swallowing the fish they catch when they dive. After they return to the boat, the fisherman takes the fish from the bird's throat and sends it off again.

In the 11th century the Chinese learnt how to bake their pottery at temperatures high enough to produce porcelain (very fine, thin and hard). When this pottery came to Europe it was called 'china' and that was the name kept when European potters learned how to make it themselves.

Paper and movable type were invented in China hundreds of years before they were used in Europe. Movable type was invented in 1041 by Pi Sheng. He carved Chinese characters onto clay blocks, then made up one page. He then reassembled the blocks ready for the next page. Eventually movable type metal printing came about in the 1200s.

Ürümqi

C

Mount Ev
29,035 ft
8,850 m

Harbin

Changchun

Amur

Beijing ▣

Yumen

Huang He

Lanzhou

Xi'an

H   I   N   A

Nanjing

Shanghai

Wuhan

Chang Jiang

Nanchang

Guangzhou

Taiwan

Kunming

Hong Kong

0	600	1200	1800	2400 miles
0	1000	2000	3000	4000 kilometres

Q&A

Q: Do the Chinese have an alphabet?

A: No. Each word has its own unique symbol or character (left). It is a system that goes back 3,600 years. It has helped the different groups of Chinese to understand each other because, although they speak many types of language, the written form can be understood by all. Traditionally, the Chinese have written vertically in columns arranged from right to left.

Q: Is rice the main food staple in China?

A: It is in the south, but in the north the Chinese people eat more wheat-based products, such as noodles or steamed buns.

Chinese Calendar and New Year

Chinese New Year is a very important holiday in China. It is celebrated in late January to early February (depending on the year). Chinese New Year starts on a New Moon and ends with the lantern festival (below) on the full moon 15 days later.

Unlike most calendars, the Chinese calendar, does not count the years in numbers but each year is given one of twelve animal names.

The twelve animals of the Chinese calendar are: Boar, Rat, Ox, Tiger, Hare or rabbit, Dragon, Snake, Horse, Ram or sheep, Monkey, Rooster.

DATA BANK

Longest river
Yangtze 3,964 miles (6,380 km)

Highest mountain
Mount Everest 29,035 ft (8,850 m)

Coastline
9,010 miles (14,500 km)

Climate
Tropical in south to subarctic in north.

Largest city and population
Shanghai 9,110,600

Annual income
US $6,800 or £4,000 approx. per person

Chinese agriculture

There are 329 million farmers in China, which means that about half of the country's work force works on the land. China grows more food than any other country in the world. Most of China's arable land is used to grow food crops such as rice, potatoes, millet, barley, peanuts and tea. Rice is one of the main foods in the Chinese diet, as are vegetables, noodles, soybeans, fish and meat. The Chinese eat with chopsticks, which are held in one hand.

Japan

Japan consists of four main islands – Kyushu, Hokkaido, Honshu and Shikoku. 70% of the land is covered with forested volcanic mountains, such as Mount Fuji (right). Towns and cities are squeezed into the flat lands along the coast, with very high levels of population density. Earth tremors and earthquakes are frequent.

Summers are warm and humid, while winters are mild, although snow can be heavy in the mountains and the north, – Sapporo hosted the winter Olympics in 2002. Agriculture, industry, and housing development are concentrated in the south-central part of Honshu. Japan has long been one of the world's richest nations, selling high-quality machinery, motor vehicles (Toyota, Honda, Nissan) and consumer electronics (Sony, Panasonic, JVC).

The Japanese economy is based on success in advanced manufacturing techniques. In the last 20 years, the focus has shifted from motor vehicles and shipbuilding, to lighter, high-value industries such as electronics. The service and finance sectors have also been growing rapidly.

Japanese food relies heavily on simplicity and freshness, with many dishes eaten raw. A variety of different foods, mainly in small portions served with rice, forms the most important part of a meal. Fish is very popular. Japan is famous for sushi (vinegared rice, eaten with seafood or vegetables) and sukiyaki (thin slices of meat served with vegetables, tofu and vermicelli) (right).

With no oil or natural gas and little coal, Japan relies heavily on overseas sources of energy. It has developed hydroelectric power, and in 1997, opened the world's biggest nuclear power station.

DATA BANK

Longest river
Shinano 228 miles (367 km)

Highest mountain
Mount Fuji 12,388 ft (3,776 m)

Coastline
18,486 miles (29,751 km)

Climate
Varies from tropical in south to cool temperate in north.

Largest city and population
Tokyo 12,369,000

Annual income
US $31,500 or £18,000 approx. per person

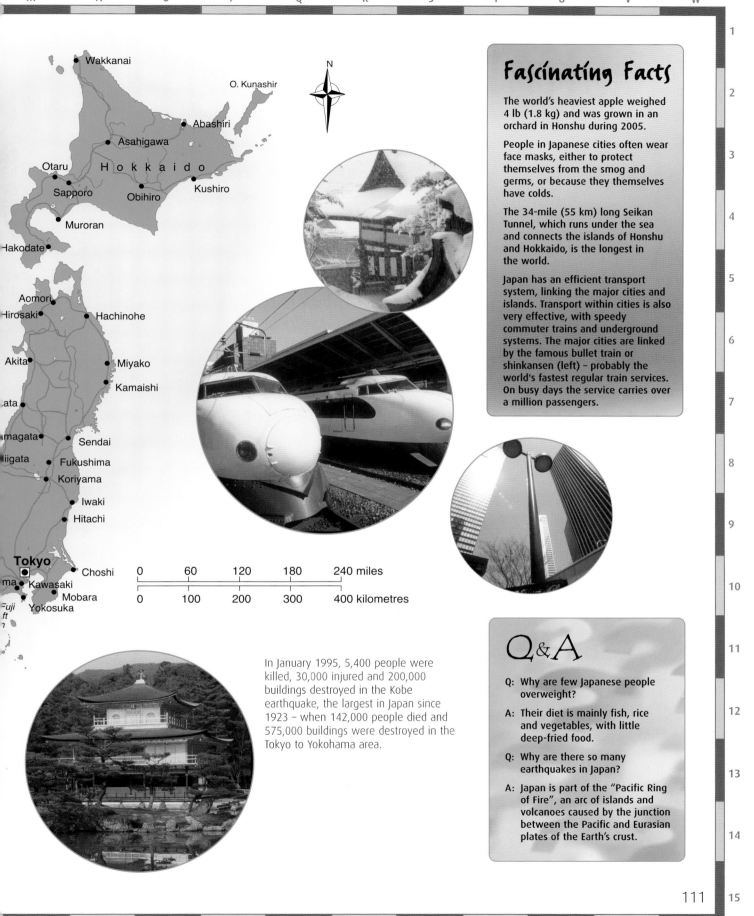

Wakkanai

O. Kunashir

Abashiri

Asahigawa

Otaru

H o k k a i d o

Sapporo

Obihiro

Kushiro

Muroran

Hakodate

Aomori

Hirosaki

Hachinohe

Akita

Miyako

Kamaishi

ata

magata

Sendai

iigata

Fukushima

Koriyama

Iwaki

Hitachi

Tokyo

Choshi

ma

Kawasaki

Mobara

Fuji
ft

Yokosuka

0   60   120   180   240 miles

0   100   200   300   400 kilometres

Fascinating Facts

The world's heaviest apple weighed 4 lb (1.8 kg) and was grown in an orchard in Honshu during 2005.

People in Japanese cities often wear face masks, either to protect themselves from the smog and germs, or because they themselves have colds.

The 34-mile (55 km) long Seikan Tunnel, which runs under the sea and connects the islands of Honshu and Hokkaido, is the longest in the world.

Japan has an efficient transport system, linking the major cities and islands. Transport within cities is also very effective, with speedy commuter trains and underground systems. The major cities are linked by the famous bullet train or shinkansen (left) – probably the world's fastest regular train services. On busy days the service carries over a million passengers.

In January 1995, 5,400 people were killed, 30,000 injured and 200,000 buildings destroyed in the Kobe earthquake, the largest in Japan since 1923 – when 142,000 people died and 575,000 buildings were destroyed in the Tokyo to Yokohama area.

Q&A

Q: Why are few Japanese people overweight?

A: Their diet is mainly fish, rice and vegetables, with little deep-fried food.

Q: Why are there so many earthquakes in Japan?

A: Japan is part of the "Pacific Ring of Fire", an arc of islands and volcanoes caused by the junction between the Pacific and Eurasian plates of the Earth's crust.

Australia-Oceania

Australia-Oceania is the smallest continent in the world. It consists of Australia, New Zealand, and a number of islands including Papua New Guinea to the north; the Solomon Islands, Vanuatu and the French dependency of New Caledonia to the northeast, and Fiji to the east.

Australia has been inhabited for over 42,000 years by native Australians. European explorers and traders started arriving in the 17th century, and in the 18th century the British claimed the eastern half of the continent as a penal (prison) colony. This area became known as New South Wales. The population grew and five more, largely self-governing states were established over the course of the 19th century. The other states are Victoria, Queensland, Northern Territory, Western Australia, and South Australia, and the island to the south of the mainland is Tasmania.

Fascinating Facts

100 years before Captain Cook arrived and claimed Australia for Britain, William Dampier (1652–1715), an English sea captain, landed on the northwest coast

Australia was not settled by Europeans until 1788 when a fleet of 11 ships bought 1,100 convicts to Sydney Cove

The giant weta is a large insect only found in New Zealand. It can grow to the size of a mouse and weigh more than 2.5 oz (70 g). This is the heaviest insect in the world (right).

Mount Wilhelm
14,793 ft
4,509 m

PAPUA NEW GUI

New

Port Moresby

INDIAN OCEAN

TIMOR SEA

Melville I.
Bathurst I.

Darwin

Groote Eylandt

Wyndham

Derby

Cairns

Northern Territory

Port Headland

Alice Springs

Queensland

A U S T R A L I A

Carnarvon

Western Australia

South Australia

Geraldton

New South Wales

Kalgoorlie-Boulder

Perth
Fremantle

Great Australian Bight

Adelaide

Ca

Albany

Kangaroo I.

Victoria

Melbourne

Geelong

| 0 | 300 | 600 | 900 | 1200 miles |

| 0 | 500 | 1000 | 1500 | 2000 kilometres |

King I.

Flinder

TASMANIA

Hobart

S O U T H E R N
O C E A N

Papua New Guinea occupies the eastern half of the island of New Guinea and numerous other islands. It is extremely diverse, with over 850 indigenous languages out of a population of just over 5 million. It is also one of the most rural, with only around 20% of people living in the towns.

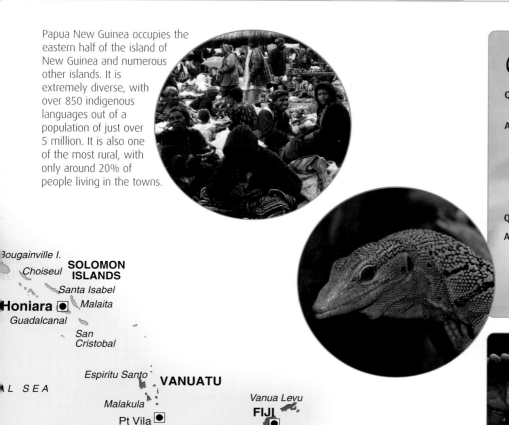

Bougainville I.
Choiseul **SOLOMON ISLANDS**
Santa Isabel
Honiara ◉ *Malaita*
Guadalcanal
San Cristobal

L SEA

Espiritu Santo **VANUATU**
Malakula
Pt Vila ◉

Vanua Levu
FIJI
Viti Levu **Suva**

NEW CALEDONIA ◉ **Nouméa**
on

ne

**P A C I F I C
O C E A N**

N

On 1 January 1901, the six colonies became a federation, and the Commonwealth of Australia was formed.

New Zealand is a country in the south-western Pacific Ocean consisting of two large islands (the North Island and South Island) and many much smaller islands. Its Maori name is Aotearoa, which translates as the 'Land of the Long White Cloud'.

New Zealand is 1,243 miles (2,000 km) from Australia – its nearest neighbours are Fiji and New Caledonia.

The population is mostly of European descent, with Maori being the largest minority group.

ASMAN SEA
North Island ● **Auckland**
NEW ZEALAND
South Island ◉ **Wellington**
● Christchurch
Stewart I.

About Australia-Oceania

The countries of Australia-Oceania, capital cities and population:

Australia	Canberra	19,978,100
Fiji	Suva	905,949
New Caledonia	Nouméa	219,246
New Zealand	Wellington	4,076,140
Papua New Guinea	Port Moresby	5,670,544
Vanuatu	Port-Vila	208,869

Industry

- In recent years Australia has become one of the world's leading wine-producing nations. The vineyards are centred in the south, near Adelaide and Perth.

- Australia has important iron and gold mining industries, mostly centred in Western Australia and supplies much of the southeast Asian region.

- Tourism is very important to any country. Television programmes and films help boost tourism, for instance, visitors flock to Melbourne to see the set of 'Neighbours', and to meet the cast.

- New Zealand is also experiencing an increase in tourism following the success of the film 'The Lord of the Rings'.

Famous people

- Sir Michael Somare (born 1936). He led Papua New Guinea to independence in 1975 and became the first prime minister.

- Dame Joan Sutherland (born 1926). One of several world-renowned opera singers to emerge from Australia.

- Kylie Minogue (born 1968). Australian star of 'Neighbours' and pop star.

- Sir Donald Bradman (1908-2001). One of Australia's (and the world's) best known cricketers.

- Sir Edmund Hillary (born 1919). He was the first person to climb Mt Everest, along with Sherpa Tenzing Norgay. Sir Edmund was a New Zealander.

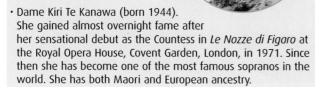

- Dame Kiri Te Kanawa (born 1944). She gained almost overnight fame after her sensational debut as the Countess in *Le Nozze di Figaro* at the Royal Opera House, Covent Garden, London, in 1971. Since then she has become one of the most famous sopranos in the world. She has both Maori and European ancestry.

Natural features

- The highest mountain in Australia is Mount Kosiuszko at 7,313 ft (2,229 m) in the Great Dividing Range in New South Wales. The ten highest mountains in Australia are within 4 miles (6 km) of each other.

- Lake Eyre in the Simpson Desert is a vast salt lake that fills with water only a few times each century.

- The most well-known natural feature is Uluru (also known as Ayers Rock) rises to 2,775 ft (846 m) and is the World's largest single piece of rock. It rises out of the completely flat desert.

- The Great Barrier Reef is a site of remarkable variety and beauty on the north-east coast of Australia. It is 1,243 miles (2,000 km) long. It contains the world's largest collection of coral reefs, with 400 types of coral and, 1,500 species of fish and 4,000 types of mollusc (animal that lives in a shell). It also holds great scientific interest as the habitat of species such as the dugong ('sea cow') and the large green turtle, both of which are threatened with extinction.

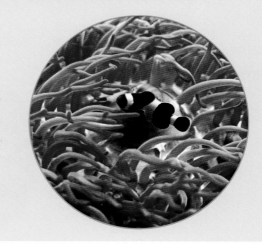

- Papua New Guinea contrasts with Australia. It is tropical and forested, and the people are much less wealthy.
- Australia is not only one of the driest countries on Earth, but it is also the lowest, having an average height of only 1,083 ft (330 m).

Languages

- Predominantly English, but many peoples from southeast Asia have arrived in recent years and Australia is now a multicultural society.
- The native population of New Zealand are the Maori. Their language is Maori or Te Reo Maori, commonly shortened to Te Reo (literally it means the language). It is an official language of New Zealand, alongside English.
- The native population of Australia is commonly called Aborigine, or Aboriginal Australian. They arrived around 50,000 BC from New Guinea when there was a land bridge connecting the two countries. They were harshly treated by the first white settlers and now maintain their own culture and language on the fringe of Australian society.
- There are over 800 languages in Papua New Guinea (also known as PNG). This is because the mountainous terrain made communication between the isolated villages very difficult. As PNG has a population of just over 5.5 million people, some languages which are spoken by very few people might soon disappear. Ten languages have already become extinct.
- New Caledonia is a French dependency called Nouvelle-Calédonie. Among the locals it is called *Kanaky*, or *Canaque* in French. The official language spoken here is French; other languages include English and German, as well as the native languages of New Caledonia, probably around 33 Melanesian-Polynesian languages and dialects.

Land use

- Most of Australia's population lives on the eastern and southern coastal fringe, as the interior is not very hospitable.
- In the outback, sheep farming is the major industry. It takes place on vast ranches, and the farmers use horses and vehicles to tend their flocks.

- New Zealand is one of the top five dairy exporters in the world. The top five countries supply around 90% of dairy products on the international market. There are over nine million beef and dairy cattle in New Zealand.

Wildlife

- The wildlife of Australia and New Zealand is unique. This means that most of the animals are not found anywhere else. They mostly belong to two animal groups: marsupials, such as kangaroos, wallabies and koalas, whose mothers carry their young in a pouch, and monotremes, such as the duck-billed platypus, which lay eggs, and produce milk to feed to their young.

- Because it was so difficult to cross the deserts in central Australia, the early settlers imported camels. Some of these escaped and became wild and are now a danger to traffic.

Australia

While a large proportion of inland Australia is desert, 40% of Australia enjoys a tropical climate and snow falls in the Australian Alps at the south end of the Great Dividing Range, or Eastern Highlands. This is Australia's most substantial range of mountains, which stretches from the north-eastern Queensland into the central plain in western Victoria.

DATA BANK

Longest river
Murray 1,566 miles (2,520 km)

Highest mountain
Mount Kosciuszko 7,313 ft (2,229 m)

Coastline
16,007 miles (25,760 km)

Climate
Very dry in centre, mild in south and east, tropical in north.

Largest city and population
Sydney 4,000,000

Annual income
US $31,900 or £18,000 approx. per person

N

Melville I.

Bathurst I.

Darwin

Gro
Eyla

Daly

Roper

Drysdale

Victoria

Broome

Fitzroy

Northern Territory

Dampier

De Grey

Barrow I.

Fortescue

A U S T R A L

Ashburton

Alice Springs

Uluru
(Ayers Rock) ▲

Finke

Carnarvon

Murchison

Western Australia

Dirk
Hartog I.

Alberga

South Australia

Laverton

Geraldton

Kalgoorlie-Boulder

Ceduna

Perth

Freemantle

Bunbury

Port Lincoln

Albany

Kangaroo I.

Mou

The Alice Springs School of the Air provides an educational service for children living in settlements covering over 386,000 sq miles (1 million sq km) of central Australia. These children live in an isolated environment, and their school classes were conducted via shortwave radio until very recently. Today most schools use wireless Internet links to receive their lessons.

Aboriginal people have lived in Australia for over 40,000 years (above left), but European settlement began in 1788 when Britain sent out 11 ships carrying around 800 convicts, landing in what is now Sydney. In 1851 gold was discovered in Victoria, and the Australian Gold Rush began.

Native Australians, known as Aborigines, were the first inhabitants of Australia. The term Aborigine includes a number of native peoples throughout Australia Oceania.

The native Australians were huntergathers; this means that they moved from place to place in search of food. They had no permanent buildings. When the Europeans arrived, many of the native people died from diseases such as smallpox. Today, many have abandoned their traditional tribal way of life and live in towns and cities, making up 1.5% of the population.

Fascinating Facts

The Great Barrier Reef, situated off the coast of Queensland, is the world's longest reef, stretching 1,243 miles (2,000 km)

The world's largest pear was grown in New South Wales in 1999. It weighed 4.6 lb (2.1 kg).

The world's fussiest eater is the Koala, which feeds exclusively on eucalyptus leaves (above right). It eats only six of the 500 species, sifting through 20 lb (9 kg) of leaves daily to find 1 lb (0.5 kg) to eat.

Although hunters have used throwing sticks in many parts of the world, the most famous of all such weapons is the Aborigines' boomerang, which may be the world's only returning throwing stick.

After the Second World War the Australian government promoted an immigration programme: over half of the migrants were British; others were Greek, German, Dutch, Italian and Yugoslav. Today over 90% of the population are of European descent; others are from Asia and the Middle East. Over 150 nationalities are represented in the population.

Canberra is Australia's capital, but Sydney is its largest city and commercial centre, as well as having the world famous Opera House (far left) and the 1,650 ft (503 m) long Sydney Harbour Bridge – which has eight lanes of roadway, two railway tracks, a cycle track and a walkway.

The Great Barrier Reef (above) is a breeding ground for green and loggerhead turtles and home to humpback whales and dolphins. Among the many fish that inhabit Australia's surrounding waters are sharks, rays and lungfish. The lungfish is unusual because it has lungs as well as a gill-breathing system. The Reef is under threat from the crown-of-thorns starfish which eats the living coral, and from rising sea levels and tourism, which damage the fragile coral ecosystem.

Q&A

Q: Was Tasmania once joined to Australia?

A: Yes, it is believed that the island was joined to the mainland until the end of the most recent ice age, about 10,000 years ago.

Q: What is a flying doctor?

A: Australians living in the outback can be far from the nearest town. The Flying Doctor service started in 1928 to provide emergency health care.

Map labels

Mitchell
Gilbert
Norman
Flinders
Cairns
Townsville
Proserpine
Mackay
Queensland
amantina
Thomson
Barcoo
Belyando
Rockhampton
Bundaberg
Fraser I.
Warrego
Toowoomba
Brisbane
Culgoa
Barwon
Grafton
Coffs Harbour
New South Wales
Darling
Lachlan
Maitland
Newcastle
Mildura
Sydney
Wagga Wagga
Wollongong
Canberra
Murray
Australian Capital Territory
Victoria
Bendigo
▲ *Mount Kosciusko 7,313 ft 2,229 m*
Ballarat
Melbourne
Geelong
King I.
Flinders I.
Cape Barren I.
Davenport
Launceston
Queenstown
TASMANIA
Hobart

0	150	300	450	600 miles
0	250	500	750	1000 kilometres

New Zealand

N[ew Zealand lies halfway between the Equator and the South Pole. It is over 1,200 miles (2,000 km) from Australia and comprises two main islands plus smaller ones. New Zealand has a thriving economy, despite its population being half that of London or New York, and it is world famous for its wines, fruit, lamb, sport and scenery.

The Maori were the first settlers. They arrived from Polynesia some time after the 13th century and established their own culture (right). New Zealand's Maori name is Aotearoa, and is usually translated as 'Land of the long white cloud', reputedly referring to the cloud the explorers saw on the horizon as they approached.

The Maori lived in fortified villages. The woodcarving used to adorn their buildings, is their main art form. Over 1,000 Maori meeting houses with intricately carved designs are still in existence. The Marae is the name for the sacred courtyard (below left), generally situated in front of the communal meeting house.

Tetaumatawhakatangihangakoauaotamate aurehaeaturipukapihimaungahoronukupok ai whenuaakitanarahu is listed in the *Guinness Book of Records* as being the longest place name in the world. It's the name of a hill in Hawkes Bay in New Zealand. It means 'The brow of the hill, where Tamatea, the man with the big knees, who slid down, climbed up and swallowed'.

Among the many sports enjoyed by New Zealanders is rafting (above). The inflatable boats hold between 4 and 12 people. It's usually carried out on white water for maximum excitement and thrill. White water means rough water, often over and around rocks, so the water looks very like foam. It usually takes place in mountainous areas, deep in the valleys. The rafters use paddles to steer the boat. Sometimes the boats are smaller, with just one or two people.

Rafting contributes to the economy of alpine regions, but there is sometimes a conflict between nature and sport. Protection of the wildlife needs to be considered, and some rivers have restrictions that limit the time of year that rafting can take place.

Fascinating Facts

The Waimangu Geyser (left) is the largest ever known. Scalding water is thrown up to 1,476 ft (450 m) into the air. In 1903 four people were killed when they were thrown 2,625 ft (800 m) by one eruption.

In 1893 New Zealand became the first country to give women the vote.

The four stars on the New Zealand flag stand for the Southern Cross constellation of stars, as seen in the sky from New Zealand.

DATA BANK

Longest river
Waikato 264 miles (425 km)

Highest mountain
Aoraki/Mount Cook 12,316 ft
(3,754 m)

Coastline
9,404 miles (15,134 km)

Climate
Mild with sharp regional contrasts

Largest city and population
Auckland 1,300,000

Annual income
US$25,200 or £14,500 approx. per
person

The first Europeans known to have reached
New Zealand arrived in 1642. Over the
years, they developed commercial farming,
and the country's industrial base. Most
people live in the cities of the warmer,
volcanic North Island, where Auckland is the
largest city and Wellington is the capital.

Christchurch is the largest city in the South
Island of New Zealand and the third largest
town in the country. It is a coastal city,
situated in the middle of the South Island's
east coast, just north of Banks Peninsula.
It is named after Christ Church, one
of the colleges at Oxford University.
Before the Europeans arrived the
area was called by the Maori
name œtautahi, probably after
the Maori chief named
Tautahi.

Whangerei

Gt. Barrier Island

Auckland

Tauranga

Hamilton

Rotorua

Waikato

Gisborne

New Plymouth

North Island

Wanganui

Napier

Hastings

Wanganui

Palmerston North

Motueka

Nelson

Blenheim

Wellington

Westport

Greymouth

South Island

Mount Cook
12,316 ft
3,754 m

Rakaia

Christchurch

Timaru

Waitaki

Oamaru

Clutha

Dunedin

Invercargill

Stewart Island

New Zealand lambs

Q&A

Q: Why are New Zealanders
called Kiwis?

A: The kiwi (above), a small
flightless bird only found in New
Zealand, has become the
country's national symbol.

Q: What is New Zealand's main
team sport?

A: Rugby. New Zealand's world-
beating international team is
known as the 'All Blacks' due to
their black shirts and shorts.

0	60	120	180	240 miles
0	100	200	300	400 kilometres

119

Antarctica
The coldest continent

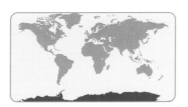

Antarctica is home to penguins, almost completely covered by ice, and is the continent that is seeing the greatest increase in temperature caused by global warming.

If the vast ice cap melts, world sea levels will rise by up to 230 ft (70 m) enough to flood London in England, New York in the USA, and almost all of Holland and Bangladesh. It would also completely submerge many islands around the world.

Who claims Antarctica

Various countries claim parts of Antarctica. These are Argentina, Australia, Chile, France, New Zealand, Norway and the United Kingdom. However in October 1991 it was agreed that no attempts would be made to discover or remove the rich minerals which lie under the ground of Antarctica. This agreements lasts until the year 2041.

Wildlife

Very little wildlife can survive the extreme conditions on the land, except various types of penguin and a few insects. The midge, just 0.5 inches (12 mm) in size, is the largest insect, and indeed the largest land animal (excluding humans). The Emperor Penguin is the only penguin to breed during the winter in Antarctica; other penguins found here are the Adélie, King, Gentoo and Chinstrap penguins (right).

In the surrounding ocean, blue whales and seals thrive, feeding on the abundant krill, a minute form of life. The fur seal was heavily hunted in the 18th and 19th centuries, but the population recovered in the 20th century. The only plants on the land are hardy mosses and lichens that can be found in some of the coastal regions.

Q&A

Q: How thick is the ice in Antarctica?

A: The ice averages 1.5 miles (2.5 km) in thickness, with the thickest ice being almost 3 miles (5 km) thick.

Q: Do polar bears live in Antarctica?

A: No. Polar bears live in the Arctic region near the North Pole, and penguins live in Antarctica, although not near the South Pole. They live nearer to the edges of the continent.

ATLANTIC OCE

Antarctic Peninsula

Ronn Ice Sh

Vinson Massif 16,860 ft 5,140 m ▲

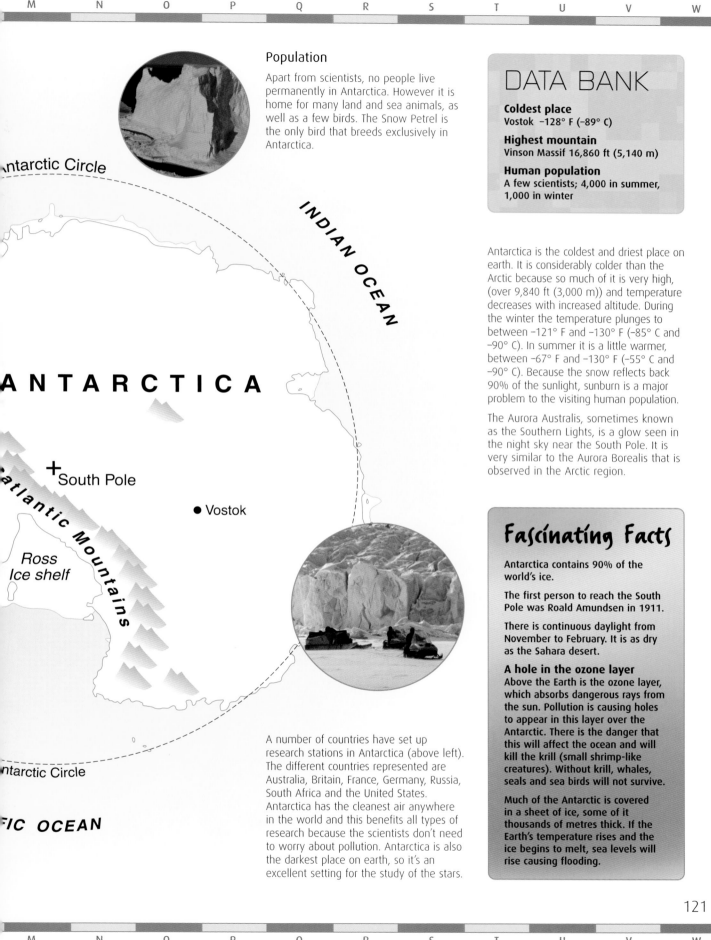

Population

Apart from scientists, no people live permanently in Antarctica. However it is home for many land and sea animals, as well as a few birds. The Snow Petrel is the only bird that breeds exclusively in Antarctica.

Antarctic Circle

INDIAN OCEAN

ANTARCTICA

+ South Pole

• Vostok

Ross Ice shelf

Atlantic Mountains

Antarctic Circle

FIC OCEAN

DATA BANK

Coldest place
Vostok −128° F (−89° C)

Highest mountain
Vinson Massif 16,860 ft (5,140 m)

Human population
A few scientists; 4,000 in summer, 1,000 in winter

Antarctica is the coldest and driest place on earth. It is considerably colder than the Arctic because so much of it is very high, (over 9,840 ft (3,000 m)) and temperature decreases with increased altitude. During the winter the temperature plunges to between −121° F and −130° F (−85° C and −90° C). In summer it is a little warmer, between −67° F and −130° F (−55° C and −90° C). Because the snow reflects back 90% of the sunlight, sunburn is a major problem to the visiting human population.

The Aurora Australis, sometimes known as the Southern Lights, is a glow seen in the night sky near the South Pole. It is very similar to the Aurora Borealis that is observed in the Arctic region.

A number of countries have set up research stations in Antarctica (above left). The different countries represented are Australia, Britain, France, Germany, Russia, South Africa and the United States. Antarctica has the cleanest air anywhere in the world and this benefits all types of research because the scientists don't need to worry about pollution. Antarctica is also the darkest place on earth, so it's an excellent setting for the study of the stars.

Fascinating Facts

Antarctica contains 90% of the world's ice.

The first person to reach the South Pole was Roald Amundsen in 1911.

There is continuous daylight from November to February. It is as dry as the Sahara desert.

A hole in the ozone layer
Above the Earth is the ozone layer, which absorbs dangerous rays from the sun. Pollution is causing holes to appear in this layer over the Antarctic. There is the danger that this will affect the ocean and will kill the krill (small shrimp-like creatures). Without krill, whales, seals and sea birds will not survive.

Much of the Antarctic is covered in a sheet of ice, some of it thousands of metres thick. If the Earth's temperature rises and the ice begins to melt, sea levels will rise causing flooding.

The Arctic
An ocean not a continent

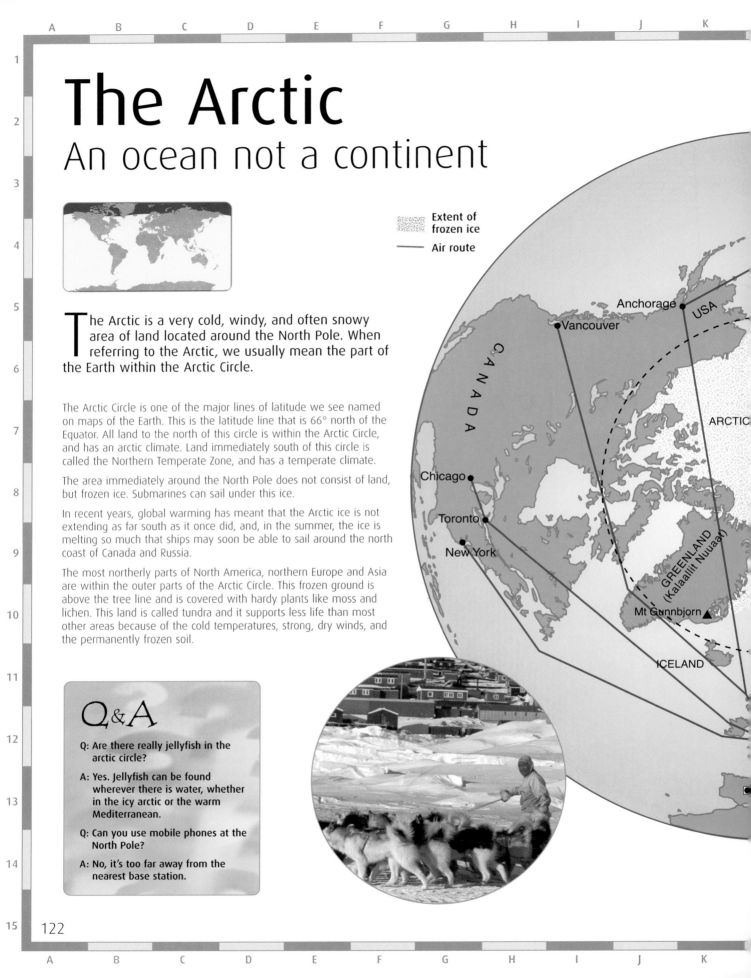

Extent of frozen ice

— **Air route**

The Arctic is a very cold, windy, and often snowy area of land located around the North Pole. When referring to the Arctic, we usually mean the part of the Earth within the Arctic Circle.

The Arctic Circle is one of the major lines of latitude we see named on maps of the Earth. This is the latitude line that is 66° north of the Equator. All land to the north of this circle is within the Arctic Circle, and has an arctic climate. Land immediately south of this circle is called the Northern Temperate Zone, and has a temperate climate.

The area immediately around the North Pole does not consist of land, but frozen ice. Submarines can sail under this ice.

In recent years, global warming has meant that the Arctic ice is not extending as far south as it once did, and, in the summer, the ice is melting so much that ships may soon be able to sail around the north coast of Canada and Russia.

The most northerly parts of North America, northern Europe and Asia are within the outer parts of the Arctic Circle. This frozen ground is above the tree line and is covered with hardy plants like moss and lichen. This land is called tundra and it supports less life than most other areas because of the cold temperatures, strong, dry winds, and the permanently frozen soil.

Q&A

Q: Are there really jellyfish in the arctic circle?

A: Yes. Jellyfish can be found wherever there is water, whether in the icy arctic or the warm Mediterranean.

Q: Can you use mobile phones at the North Pole?

A: No, it's too far away from the nearest base station.

Anchorage

Vancouver

CANADA

ARCTIC

Chicago

Toronto

New York

GREENLAND
(Kalaallit Nuuaat)

Mt Gunnbjorn ▲

ICELAND

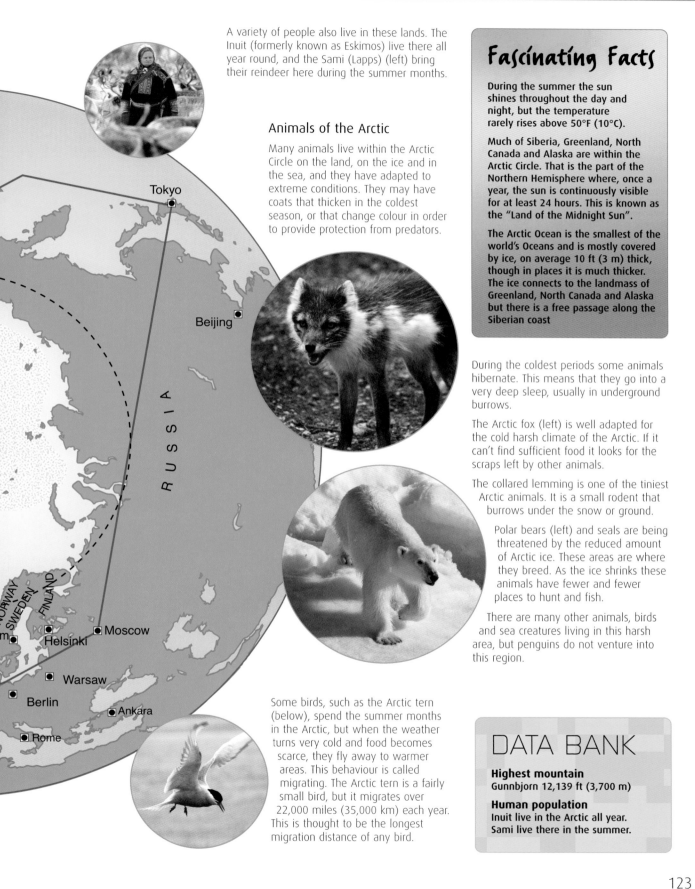

A variety of people also live in these lands. The Inuit (formerly known as Eskimos) live there all year round, and the Sami (Lapps) (left) bring their reindeer here during the summer months.

Animals of the Arctic

Many animals live within the Arctic Circle on the land, on the ice and in the sea, and they have adapted to extreme conditions. They may have coats that thicken in the coldest season, or that change colour in order to provide protection from predators.

Tokyo

Beijing

R U S S I A

NORWAY
SWEDEN
FINLAND
olm
Helsinki
Moscow

Warsaw

Berlin
Ankara
Rome

Some birds, such as the Arctic tern (below), spend the summer months in the Arctic, but when the weather turns very cold and food becomes scarce, they fly away to warmer areas. This behaviour is called migrating. The Arctic tern is a fairly small bird, but it migrates over 22,000 miles (35,000 km) each year. This is thought to be the longest migration distance of any bird.

Fascinating Facts

During the summer the sun shines throughout the day and night, but the temperature rarely rises above 50°F (10°C).

Much of Siberia, Greenland, North Canada and Alaska are within the Arctic Circle. That is the part of the Northern Hemisphere where, once a year, the sun is continuously visible for at least 24 hours. This is known as the "Land of the Midnight Sun".

The Arctic Ocean is the smallest of the world's Oceans and is mostly covered by ice, on average 10 ft (3 m) thick, though in places it is much thicker. The ice connects to the landmass of Greenland, North Canada and Alaska but there is a free passage along the Siberian coast

During the coldest periods some animals hibernate. This means that they go into a very deep sleep, usually in underground burrows.

The Arctic fox (left) is well adapted for the cold harsh climate of the Arctic. If it can't find sufficient food it looks for the scraps left by other animals.

The collared lemming is one of the tiniest Arctic animals. It is a small rodent that burrows under the snow or ground.

Polar bears (left) and seals are being threatened by the reduced amount of Arctic ice. These areas are where they breed. As the ice shrinks these animals have fewer and fewer places to hunt and fish.

There are many other animals, birds and sea creatures living in this harsh area, but penguins do not venture into this region.

DATA BANK

Highest mountain
Gunnbjorn 12,139 ft (3,700 m)

Human population
Inuit live in the Arctic all year.
Sami live there in the summer.

Index

M

Macedonia, Europe	51	P11
Mackenzie Mountains, Canada	64	I6
Mackenzie, *River*, North America	64	F6
Madagascar, *Island*, Africa	91	R7
Madeira, *Island*, North Atlantic Ocean	12	L7
Madrid, Spain	45	M10
Maine, United States of America	67	U3
Malabo, Equatorial Guinea	86	F5
Malawi, Africa	89	N13
Malaysia, Asia	106	G11
Maldives, *Islands*, Indian Ocean	13	P8
Mali, Africa	82	I8
Malta, *Island*, Europe	22	K13
Managua, Nicaragua	74	K5
Manchester, England	27	S10
Manila, Philippines	107	L7
Manitoba, Canada	65	L8
Maputo, Mozambique	90	L10
Marshall Islands, North Pacific Ocean	13	U8
Maryland, United States of America	71	U3
Maseru, Lesotho	90	J12
Massachusetts, United States of America	67	U4
Mauritania, Africa	82	E8
Mauritius, *Island*, Indian Ocean	13	O9
Mbabane, Swaziland	90	L10
Mediterranean Sea	15	M7
Mekong, *River*, Asia	15	Q8
Mexico, North America	73	M6
Mexico City, Mexico	73	N9
Michigan, United States of America	67	Q5
Minnesota, United States of America	67	O4
Minsk, Belarus	52	K10
Mississippi, *River*, North America	14	H7
Missouri, *River*, North America	14	H7
Missouri, United States of America	67	P7
Moldova, Europe	52	L12
Mongolia, Asia	92	K8
Monrovia, Liberia	84	H10
Montana, United States of America	69	P3
Montenegro, Europe	51	N9
Montevideo, Uruguay	75	O11
Morocco, Africa	82	H5
Moscow, Russia	53	M8
Mount Aconcagua, Argentina	14	I11
Mount Elbrus, Russia	15	O7
Mount Everest, Asia	15	Q8
Mount Kilimanjaro, Tanzania	15	N9
Mount McKinley, United States of America	15	V6
Mount Wilhelm, Papua New Guinea	15	S10
Mozambique, Africa	91	M9
Murray, *River*, Australia	15	S11
Muscat, Oman	101	R9
Myanmar, Asia	106	E7

N

Nairobi, Kenya	89	N9
Namibia, Africa	90	F8
Ndjamena, Chad	83	M11
Nebraska, United States of America	67	N6
Nepal, Asia	105	M5
Netherlands, Europe	33	M6
Nevada, United States of America	69	N9
New Brunswick, Canada	65	Q9
New Caledonia, *Islands*, Australasia	113	N8
New Hampshire, United States of America	67	U4
New Jersey, United States of America	71	V1
New Mexico, United States of America	67	L8
New South Wales, Australia	117	N11
New York, United States of America	67	S5
New Zealand, Australasia	113	N13
Newfoundland, Canada	65	P8
Niamey, Niger	82	J10
Nicaragua, Central America	74	K5
Nicosia, Cyprus	23	N13

Niger, Africa	82	K9
Niger, *River*, Africa	15	M8
Nigeria, Africa	85	M10
Nile, *River*, Africa	15	N8
North America, *Continent*	60	K7
North Atlantic Ocean	14	K7
North Carolina, United States of America	71	T5
North Dakota, United States of America	67	M4
North Island, New Zealand	119	T6
North Korea, Asia	93	N9
North Pacific Ocean	14	E7
North Sea, Europe	22	I9
Northern Ireland, United Kingdom	27	P9
Northern Territories, Canada	64	K7
Northern Territory, Australia	116	J7
Norway, Europe	31	N8
Norwegian Sea, Europe	15	L6
Nouakchott, Mauritania	82	E8
Nouméa, New Caledonia	113	O8
Nova Scotia, Canada	65	Q10
Nuuk, Greenland	61	P5

O

Oceania *see* Australasia		
Ohio, United States of America	71	Q2
Oklahoma, United States of America	67	N8
Oman, Asia	101	Q11
Ontario, Canada	65	M9
Oregon, United States of America	68	K5
Orkney Islands, Scotland	27	R3
Oslo, Norway	31	O10
Ottawa, Canada	65	P10
Ouagadougou, Burkino Faso	84	K9
Outer Hebrides, *Islands*, Scotland	27	P4

P

Pakistan, Asia	104	G5
Panama, Central America	74	K5
Panama City, Panama	74	L5
Papua New Guinea, Australasia	112	J5
Paraguay, South America	75	N9
Paramaribo, Suriname	75	O6
Paris, France	35	N4
Pennsylvania, United States of America	71	S1
Peru, South America	75	L8
Philippine Sea, Asia	15	S8
Philippines, Asia	107	M7
Phnom Penh, Cambodia	106	H9
Poland, Europe	49	M6
Port Moresby, Papua New Guinea	112	J6
Port Vila, Vanuatu	113	O7
Porto Novo, Benin	84	L10
Portugal, Europe	46	J9
Prague, Czech Republic	48	J9
Pretoria, South Africa	90	K10
Puerto Rico, Central America	12	I8
Pyongyang, North Korea	93	N9
Pyrenees, *Mountains*, Europe	34	K10

Q

Qatar, Asia	101	O8
Quebec, Canada	65	O9
Queensland, Australia	117	M8
Quibd, Colombia	75	L6
Quinto, Ecuador	74	L6

R

Rabat, Morocco	82	H4
Red Sea, Africa/Asia	83	S7
Republic of Ireland, Europe	27	N11
Reykjavik, Iceland	22	E7
Rhine, *River*, Europe	15	M6
Rhode Island, United States of America	67	U5
Riga, Latvia	52	J8
Rio Grande, *River*, North America	14	H8
Riyadh, Saudi Arabia	101	M9
Rocky Mountains, North America	14	F6

ACKNOWLEDGMENTS

The authors and publishers would like to thank the following people
who played such a significant role in creating this Children's Atlas:

Illustration
HL Studios

Page Design
HL Studios

Editorial
Ros Morley, Lucie Williams

Photo research
Ros Morley

Project management
HL Studios

Jacket Design
JPX

Production
Elaine Ward